# HEALTHY
# EASY
# MEXICAN

# HEALTHY EASY MEXICAN

### OVER 140 AUTHENTIC
## LOW-CALORIE, BIG-FLAVOR
### RECIPES

## VELDA DE LA GARZA, MS, RDN

### PHOTOGRAPHY BY JUSTIN WALKER

THE EXPERIMENT

NEW YORK

HEALTHY EASY MEXICAN: *Over 140 Authentic Low-Calorie, Big-Flavor Recipes*
Text, and photographs on pages 10, 11, 98, and 241, copyright © 1995, 2021 by Velda de la Garza, MS, RDN
Photographs copyright © 2021 by Justin Walker

Originally published as *Healthy Mexican Cooking: Authentic Low-Fat Recipes* by Appletree Press in 1995.
First published in revised form by The Experiment, LLC, in 2021.

The Experiment, LLC | 220 East 23rd Street, Suite 600 | New York, NY 10010-4658
theexperimentpublishing.com

This book contains the opinions and ideas of its author. It is intended to provide helpful and informative material on the subjects addressed in the book. It is sold with the understanding that the author and publisher are not engaged in rendering medical, health, or any other kind of personal professional services in the book. The author and publisher specifically disclaim all responsibility for any liability, loss, or risk—personal or otherwise—that is incurred as a consequence, directly or indirectly, of the use and application of any of the contents of this book.

THE EXPERIMENT and its colphon are registered trademarks of The Experiment, LLC. Many of the designations used by manufacturers and sellers to distinguish their products are claimed as trademarks. Where those designations appear in this book and The Experiment was aware of a trademark claim, the designations have been capitalized.

The Experiment's books are available at special discounts when purchased in bulk for premiums and sales promotions as well as for fund-raising or educational use. For details, contact us at info@theexperimentpublishing.com.

Library of Congress Cataloging-in-Publication Data

Names: De la Garza, Velda, author.
Title: Healthy easy Mexican : 140 authentic low-calorie, big-flavor recipes
  / Velda de la Garza, MS, RDN.
Description: 2nd edition. | New York : The Experiment, [2021] | Includes
  index.
Identifiers: LCCN 2021016432 (print) | LCCN 2021016433 (ebook) | ISBN
  9781615197606 | ISBN 9781615197613 (eISBN)
Subjects: LCSH: Cooking, Mexican. | Low-fat diet--Recipes.
Classification: LCC TX716.M4 L34 2021  (print) | LCC TX716.M4  (ebook) |
  DDC 641.5972--dc23
LC record available at https://lccn.loc.gov/2021016432
LC ebook record available at https://lccn.loc.gov/2021016433

ISBN 978-1-61519-760-6
Ebook ISBN 978-1-61519-761-3

Cover and text design by Beth Bugler
Food styling by Veronica Spera
Author photograph by Diana Cantu

Manufactured in China

First printing September 2021
10 9 8 7 6 5 4 3 2 1

# HEALTHY
# EASY
# MEXICAN

# CONTENTS

# INTRODUCTION

Food is such a vital part of our Mexican heritage. We use food to celebrate the important stages of our lives. From baptisms to weddings to wakes, food forms the glue of life that brings us together and binds us as families and friends. Many deep-rooted traditions go along with the ever-so-satisfying food that represents our culture. Even our Aztec ancestors were known to have prepared tamales using wild game in the 1500s.

In recent years, Mexican food has become one of the most popular cuisines in the United States. It's often diverse, differing with each geographic area. Hatch chiles are incorporated into many dishes in New Mexico; in Texas, Anaheim and ancho chiles are more often used. In California, strawberry and pineapple tamales are popular, but they're much less common in Texas. California tamales are meal-sized concoctions; in Texas, you would likely consume two or three smaller ones as part of a meal. Carnitas are very popular in California, and not as common in Texas. Many of these foods are variations of the same basic ingredients, such as enchiladas, prepared with different regional touches.

The recipes in this book are the type I enjoy preparing—few ingredients, short preparation times, and lower in calories than many traditional preparations. Many of the recipes I learned to cook at home with my mother, some are from my husband's family, and others are from friends. Some are recipes I've collected while living in different parts of the country. Though I prepare them by incorporating newer food trends, these recipes are still representative of hundreds of years of history and culture. They maintain their tradition in our families, despite borders, economics, and the passing of time.

This cookbook shows that many of our traditional recipes can be modified to be

healthier and still taste great. In most of the recipes, the amounts of seasoning and vegetables—bay leaves, cilantro, epazote, garlic, and onions—have been increased to add flavor without too many additional calories.

Many of our traditional foods are naturally healthy. We enjoy so many variations of salsas, such as Salsa Ranchera (page 33) and Salsa de Tomatillo Tatemado (page 44), which are made with vegetables. We have our refreshing aguas frescas (Agua Fresca de Sandía, page 236), made with whole fruits and even vegetables. Numerous recipes, such as Dip con Frijol Negro y Elote (page 54) incorporate vitamin- and fiber-rich ingredients such as salsas, corn, and beans.

Avocados are a key ingredient in Mexican dishes. They are considered a superfood because they contain so many powerful nutrients and phytochemicals. They're also a good source of monounsaturated fats, which can help lower cholesterol levels and reduce inflammation. Avocados can be eaten as a simple meal, wrapped in a warm, fresh tortilla (Tortillas de Maíz, page 105), used as a wonderful garnish in tacos, or incorporated into a delightful sauce or salsa (Crema de Aguacate, page 47; Guacamole con Comino Tostado, page 49).

Legumes, such as beans and lentils (also considered superfoods), have always been important staples in our diets. Lentils can be prepared with Mexican seasonings (Especias Mexicanas, page 24), which add a wonderful flavor. There are hundreds of delicious ways to prepare pinto and black beans (Frijoles de Olla, page 223; Frijoles Negros, page 225).

· · · · · · · · · · · · · · · · · · · · · · · · · · · · · **HEALTHY EASY MEXICAN** · · · · · · · · · · · · · · · · · · · · · · · · · ·

10

There are also countless options for meatless meals with Mexican flavors. These can be as simple as pinto beans combined with rice or corn, which make for a complete and healthy (not to mention cost-effective) meal. Tostadas (such as Tostadas de Frijol y Queso, page 198), enchiladas (such as Enchiladas de Chile Colorado, page 199), Entomatadas (page 200), and even nachos (such as Nachos con Frijoles, Queso y Aguacate, page 62) can make delectable complete meals without using meat.

Cheese is another common ingredient in Mexican foods. Many of the recipes in this book incorporate cheese, but I recommend those that are lower in fat, such as reduced-fat cheddar, American, and Monterey Jack cheeses. Many Mexican cheeses are made with part-skim milk and are delicious when combined with the stronger flavors of foods such as enchiladas. Some recipes call for full-fat cheeses in smaller quantities, which is also acceptable when used occasionally.

Your journey to good health should start in the kitchen. Stock your kitchen with an abundance of fruits and vegetables, nuts, legumes, reduced-fat dairy, and lean proteins. Use vegetable oils in your cooking instead of animal fats, and learn

healthy cooking methods to improve your meals. Learning about nutrition and incorporating that knowledge into your cooking is the most important investment you can make for your health. Taking steps to have a healthy kitchen is easy—and this book can help.

By preparing food at home, we control what ingredients go into our food as well as how much of that food we consume, which can help us stay healthy. Though the recipes in this book are not specifically for diabetes, they are, except for some desserts, within diabetic guidelines. Some of the recipes, such as for Empanadas de Manzana (page 253), can be further modified with sugar alternatives. Most of the foods are moderate in sodium, following general guidelines for good health. If your physician has recommended decreasing your salt intake for medical reasons, many of these recipes can be adapted with low-sodium products.

This food represents our beautiful Mexican customs that go back hundreds of years. It makes us feel comforted and at home. Use my recipes as inspiration to build your own healthy Mexican dishes. I hope you enjoy these recipes as much as I do.

*¡Buen provecho!*

# HEALTHY EATING GUIDELINES

**F**ood can bring us joy, comfort, and pleasure. But it's also the most powerful tool we have in achieving and maintaining good health. The association between our food choices and our health has never been clearer. And although the science regarding our food and our health is ever-evolving, many of the principles remain unchanged.

Eating a diet that follows healthy eating guidelines can help to prevent high blood pressure, diabetes, cardiovascular disease, and certain types of cancer. The following guidelines have been developed by the United States Department of Agriculture (USDA) and Health and Human Services (HHS) and are backed by extensive research.*

The 2020 to 2025 *Dietary Guidelines for Americans* stress the inclusion of "nutrient-dense" foods. These foods have little or no added sugars, saturated fat, or sodium but contain vitamins, minerals, and other essential nutrients.

Their recommendations include:

- **Eat more vegetables.** Whole vegetables are best, and vegetables richer in color typically have the most nutrients, vitamins, minerals, and antioxidants. For example, a sweet potato has more nutrients than a white potato. Kale has more nutrients than iceberg lettuce. All vegetables have merit in our diet, but to get the most from your food, choose those with deep color.

- **Eat more fruits, especially whole fruits.** Richly colored fruits contain phytonutrients, chemicals produced by plants, which have antioxidant and anti-inflammatory properties. Fresh fruits are a better choice; if you choose canned fruits, select those canned in their own juice. Frozen fruits without sugar are also a healthy choice.

- **Eat more whole grains.** These include whole wheat cereals, whole wheat bread and tortillas, brown rice, and

* US Department of Agriculture and US Department of Health and Human Services, *Dietary Guidelines for Americans, 2020-2025*, 9th ed. (Washington, DC: USDA/HHS, 2020), dietaryguidelines.gov.

oats. Whole grains contain more fiber, B vitamins, and minerals, such as iron and magnesium.

- **Eat dairy products that are fat-free or low-fat.** This includes milk, cheese, yogurt, and alternative dairy beverages, such as fortified soy beverages. Although the evidence is still emerging on the role of dairy fats in our diet, full-fat dairy products do contain more calories than their reduced-fat counterparts.

- **Eat a variety of proteins, including seafood, skinless poultry, lean meats, eggs, legumes, nuts, seeds, and soy products.** Consume nuts in small quantities, lightly salted, if possible. Eat seafood, especially tuna, mackerel, and salmon, twice a week.

- **Consume less sodium.** Many fast foods and processed foods have high amounts of sodium, so cooking your own food is the best way to keep your sodium intake down. Limit sodium intake to less than 2,300 milligrams per day. One fast food meal can often give you more than half of your recommended sodium intake.

- **Consume alcohol in moderation.** Limit to one drink per day for women and two drinks per day for men.

- **Incorporate oils into your diet, including vegetable oils and oils in foods like nuts and seafood.** Substitute oils for fats that are solid at room temperature, such as shortening and lard.

- **Limit sugars**. Sugars are found in many forms in our processed foods and especially in soft drinks. One teaspoon of sugar contains 4 grams, and one 12-ounce (350 ml) soft drink can have about 10 teaspoons of sugar (or 40 grams!). Added sugars should make up less than 10 percent of your daily calories. If you consume 1,800 calories, that means no more than 180 calories should come from sugar.

- **Cut back on saturated fat.** Most saturated fats come from animal sources (meat and dairy), though they can also be found in tropical oils, such as palm oil and coconut oil. Less than 10 percent of your daily calories should come from saturated fat.

# A WORD ABOUT FATS

Since it can sometimes be confusing to navigate the recommendations regarding fats, here's a more in-depth guide to the different types.

**Saturated fats** are almost always solid or waxy at room temperature. They include many animal fats, full-fat and even some reduced-fat dairy products, palm oil, and coconut oil. Many saturated fats are believed to increase cholesterol and therefore contribute to cardiovascular disease.

**Trans fats** are chemically changed from liquid to solid fat—they are often added to processed foods or used to fry fast foods. Trans fats elevate "bad" cholesterol (LDL) and decrease "good" cholesterol (HDL), so it's best to avoid them. Look out for "hydrogenated" or "partially hydrogenated" on nutrition labels.

**Polyunsaturated fats,** almost always liquid at room temperature, are mostly derived from plant sources. They include canola oil, corn oil, grapeseed oil, safflower oil, sesame oil, and sunflower oil. They also include omega-3 fatty acids, which are found in salmon, mackerel, sardines, albacore tuna, and some vegetables, legumes, nuts, and seeds. Albondigas de Salmón (page 152) are simple to prepare and rich in omega-3 fatty acids.

**Monounsaturated fats** are derived from plants. The best sources include olive oil, canola oil, high-oleic safflower oil, peanut oil, avocados, and peanuts, as well as other nuts and seeds. Monounsaturated fats are known to reduce cholesterol. To add more monounsaturated fats to your diet, try Guacamole con Comino Tostado (page 49), Ensalada de Aguacate y Toronja (page 117), and Ensalada de Repollo con Aderezo de Aguacate (page 120).

A healthy diet contains oils derived primarily from plant sources, like olive and canola oils. Fats have more than double the calories of the other main nutrients—carbohydrates and proteins—so keep in mind that calories from fats add up rather fast. The quality of fat you consume matters, but so does the quantity. This book contains many recipes to help you find that balance.

*Que tus alimentos sean tus medicinas.* May your food be your medicine.

# AT THE GROCERY STORE

With so many choices available at the grocery store, buying groceries can be confusing, but it is easy to remember that some of the best nutritional choices are found around the perimeter of the grocery store. Fresh fruits and vegetables, reduced-fat milk products, lean meats, and reduced-fat cheeses can all be found on the outside aisles of the supermarket. Frozen vegetables and unsweetened fruit juices are also good choices.

When going through aisles with candies, cookies, pastries, and ice creams, just say no. Opt for simpler, less-processed, lower-calorie foods.

| TRY | INSTEAD OF |
| --- | --- |
| Corn tortillas, whole wheat tortillas made with oil, whole wheat pita bread, 100 percent whole wheat bread, whole wheat bolillos | Flour tortillas, rich breads, rolls |
| Lean beef, chicken breast, pork loin, soy and legume patties | Organ meats, high-fat meats such as brisket, pork shoulder, hot dogs, bacon |
| Lean ground beef (90 to 95 percent lean) or ground turkey breast | Regular ground beef |
| Skim or low-fat milk | Whole milk |
| Reduced-fat cream cheese, Greek cream cheese, neufchatel cream cheese | Cream cheese |
| Reduced-fat cheese, string cheese, part-skim Mexican cheeses such as panela, queso fresco, and queso blanco | Regular cheese |
| Greek yogurt, low-fat plain yogurt, reduced-fat sour cream | Sour cream |
| Pinto beans, black beans, kidney beans, lentils, nonfat refried beans made with oil | Refried beans made with lard |

· · · · · · · · · · · · · · · · · · · · · · · · HEALTHY EATING GUIDLINES · · · · · · · · · · · · · · · · · · · · · · · ·

15

| TRY | INSTEAD OF |
|---|---|
| Mayonnaise made with olive oil, reduced-calorie mayonnaise and salad dressings | Mayonnaise or creamy salad dressings |
| Liquid margarine or margarine with plant sterols, butter blended with olive or canola oil | Stick margarine, butter |
| Liquid vegetable oils, such as olive and canola | Shortening or lard; coconut, palm, cottonseed, and palm kernel oils |
| Fruits, fresh or canned in their own juice | Fruits canned in heavy syrup |
| Baked tortilla chips | Fried tortilla chips |
| High-fiber cereal with 5 grams or more fiber per serving | Sugar-rich, low-fiber cereals |
| Brown rice, whole wheat pasta | White rice, pasta |
| Pretzels, baked chips, or air-popped corn | Chips |
| Animal or graham crackers | Cookies |
| Frozen yogurt or reduced-fat ice cream, frozen fruit bars | Gourmet ice cream |
| Sugar-free gelatin | Regular desserts or gelatin |
| 100 percent fruit juice | Sugary beverages |

| FAT SOURCES TO USE | FAT SOURCES TO AVOID/USE LESS |
|---|---|
| Olive oil | Lard, bacon fat |
| Canola oil | Beef, pork, veal, lamb, poultry fat |
| Vegetable and nut oils | Coconut oil, palm oil |
| Trans fat–free and cholesterol-lowering margarines, butter blended with olive oil | Hydrogenated margarine and shortening |
| Avocados, nuts and seeds | Butter |

Here are some guidelines for buying meat at the grocery store.

- Purchase flank steak instead of skirt steak, since it's leaner.

- Brisket, choice, and prime cuts of beef are all high-fat meats.

- Avoid all organ meats. This includes liver, brains, sweetbreads, tripe, and tongue.

- The fat content of turkey is usually not labeled. Ground turkey is usually a combination of white and dark meats, skin, and fat. Look for ground turkey breast, since it's leaner.

- All chicken parts have different fat contents. The breast is the lowest in fat, followed by the drumstick and then the thigh. Remember to always remove all skin and excess fat before cooking.

The following are better choices of meats to purchase.

Key words to remember are "round" or "loin" for beef, and "loin" or "leg" for pork, lamb, and veal. These words on the label indicate a lower fat content. Try to purchase "select" cuts of beef. This term indicates a lower fat content. Even when cooking lean meat, drain off excess juices and fat.

**Beef:** round tip, top round, eye of round, top loin, tenderloin, and sirloin

**Pork:** tenderloin, boneless top loin, center loin chop

**Poultry:** chicken breast, skinless chicken leg, skinless turkey breast, skinless turkey dark meat (Removing the skin before preparing reduces fat content.)

**Lamb:** loin, chop, leg

**Fish:** fresh or frozen fish or canned fish packed in water (Fish containing omega-3 fatty acids include mackerel, salmon, and tuna.)

La Cocina Mexicana

# THE MEXICAN KITCHEN: TOOLS, TIPS, AND INGREDIENTS

## TOOLS

Having the right equipment can make all the difference when cooking authentic Mexican cuisine.

### Griddle

Nice, but not absolutely necessary for making corn tortillas (Tortillas de Maíz, page 105) or flour tortillas (Tortillas de Harina, page 109; Tortillas de Trigo Integral, page 110). Electric griddles heat more evenly and cook more tortillas at a time than other griddles or pans, but stovetop griddles or good-quality pans also work well.

### Molcajete

Made of lava rock, the molcajete functions as a mortar and pestle for grinding spices, such as cumin seeds, peppercorns, and garlic. The rough rock texture is excellent for grinding spices. If you don't have access to a molcajete, a blender or spice grinder can be used to grind spices as well.

### Nonstick pan/skillet

Essential for a healthy kitchen. Using nonstick pans helps decrease the total amount of fat used in cooking. When using nonstick pans, reduce the heating temperature slightly to avoid scorching foods. Good-quality pans are an excellent investment and can last for many years.

**Rolling pin**
For flour tortilla preparation (Tortillas de Harina, page 109; Tortillas de Trigo Integral, page 110).

**Tortilla press**
For corn tortillas (Tortillas de Maíz, page 105). The tortilla press consists of two hinged metal circles, preferably cast iron, 6 to 8 inches (15 to 20 cm) in diameter with a lever opposite the hinge. Corn masa (dough) is placed in the center of the press, and one side is lowered using the lever to flatten the dough and form the tortilla. If you don't have access to a tortilla press, you can also use your hands to form corn tortillas.

**Tortilla warmer**
Insulated round container with a tight-fitting lid to keep tortillas warm until you're ready to eat them. Insulated cloth tortilla warmers are easy to store and work quite well.

# TIPS

- Make a batch of Mexican Spice Blend (Especias Mexicanas, page 24) to keep on hand. Use a molcajete, blender, or spice grinder to grind garlic, cumin, and peppercorns, then mix with a small amount of water. This will keep for about fourteen days in the refrigerator and can be frozen in an ice cube tray for up to six months.

- Most of the recipes in this book use olive or canola oil for frying or sautéing instead of shortening or lard. Use butter sparingly (I like Land O'Lakes butter with olive oil).

- Refried beans don't have to be fried! To make my Unfried Refried Beans (Frijoles Refritos sin Freir, page 224), cook your beans, drain them slightly, and use a potato masher to achieve a thick consistency. Allow any excess liquid to evaporate by simmering them gently. These beans can be prepared using a small amount of olive oil.

- Corn tortillas (Tortillas de Maíz, page 105) are the healthiest tortilla option, since they have fewer calories than flour tortillas (Tortillas de Harina, page 109). They are made with masa harina (flour made from treated corn) and are low in sodium when made without added salt. Whole wheat tortillas (Tortillas de Trigo Integral, page 110), made with olive or canola oil, are another healthy choice, since they contain more fiber, vitamins, and minerals than their white-flour counterparts.

- Use baked tortillas for making tostadas (Tostadas de Frijol y Queso, page 198), chips (Tortillas Doradas, page 107), and tacos (Tacos de Puerco Pernil, page 149; Tacos de Pavo con Frijoles y Chile, page 186). Tortillas can also be grilled until crisp and lightly toasted—dip these in the salsa of your choice.

- Homemade salsas enhance the flavors of many foods and add necessary vitamins to your diet. Tomatoes and chiles are good sources of vitamins A and C, and most salsas are low in calories. Homemade salsas are also lower in sodium than store-bought salsas.

- When preparing *guisados* (braised meat stews), remove all skin and excess fat from meats. Sauté over medium heat in olive or other vegetable oil.

- Experiment with different reduced-fat cheeses (see page 22). Or mix reduced-fat cheese with a small quantity of full-fat cheese. When baking with reduced-fat cheeses, such as in my Pollo Rancho King recipe (page 172), add them about 10 minutes before the end of baking time to prevent them from drying out.

- Adding fresh vegetables to beans, rice, and noodles will add more fiber and vitamins, such as vitamins A, K, and C, to your meals.

- Prepare rice and pasta dishes with olive oil or other vegetable oils. Try whole wheat pasta and brown rice for healthier options with more fiber. Brown rice can be substituted for white rice in most Mexican rice dishes, but be sure to increase the liquid and cooking time. Mexican rice can also be prepared by steaming rice instead of frying it. You can even substitute cauliflower rice for a lower-carb option.

- When preparing guacamole (Guacamole con Comino Tostado, page 49), add fresh fruits and vegetables, such as onions, tomatoes, garlic, and lime juice, to increase the fiber and add vitamins. You can also prepare a wonderful creamy avocado sauce with Greek yogurt (Crema de Aguacate, page 47).

- When cooking pinto beans, there's no need to add lots of salt pork or bacon. Instead, try adding one slice of bacon and a small amount of olive oil to give the beans more flavor, without the excess fat. I keep individual rolled-up strips of bacon in the freezer for easy use. Add a variety of other vegetables such as celery, carrots, onions, cilantro, and tomatoes to increase your vitamin intake.

# La Despensa Mexicana
# THE MEXICAN PANTRY

Keep these items on hand to prepare simple, healthy Mexican meals.

Avocados

Bell peppers

Black peppercorns

Broth, chicken or vegetable

Butter (I like Land O'Lakes butter with olive oil)

Cabbage

Chiles

Chili powder (I use Gebhardt's)

Cilantro

Corn (fresh or frozen)

Corn tortillas and baked tostadas

Cumin seeds

Flour, all-purpose and whole wheat

Garlic

Lettuce

Limes

Masa harina (flour made from treated corn)

Mexican Spice Blend (page 24)

Onions

Pinto beans, black beans, kidney beans, and lentils

Olive oil or vegetable oil

Reduced-fat cheeses, such as Monterey Jack, cheddar, and part-skim Mexican cheeses

Rice, brown or white

Salt

Tatuma squash and zucchini

Tomatillos

Tomatoes

Tomato sauce

## Quesos Mexicanos
# MEXICAN CHEESES

Many Mexican cheeses are made from part-skim milk, which lowers the saturated-fat content. Always read the labels to be sure, since different brands may have different fat contents. These cheeses can be used to make quesadillas (Quesadillas a la Parilla, page 65; Quesadilla de Chile, page 66) and enchiladas (Enchiladas Suizas, page 174; Enchiladas de Pollo en Salsa de Chile Ancho, page 176) and are often used as garnishes for Mexican foods.

---

**Panela**
A creamy, tangy cheese. Great with squash in Calabaza con Queso Panela (page 206). Panela cheese can be substituted for chicken in Enchiladas de Pollo en Salsa de Chile Ancho (page 176).

**Queso fresco**
A fresh, soft cow's milk cheese. It's somewhat salty, like feta. Use this cheese in my Tacos de Camote (page 195). You can also add it to salads.

**Queso blanco**
Tastes like mild ricotta. It's often crumbled over spicy Mexican dishes such as Tacos de Puerco Pernil (page 149).

**Cotija**
An aged, salty cheese used to top Mexican dishes such as Ensalada de Elote (page 132).

**Oaxaca**
A great melting cheese with a buttery flavor. It's pulled into long, ropelike strings and wound into a knot.

# CHILES

Chiles are central to Mexican cooking. They add flavor, color, and varying degrees of heat to many foods.

### Anaheim

Ranging from mild to hot in flavor, Anaheim peppers are one of the most popular varieties of chiles. When fresh, they're bright green, 4 to 5 inches (10 to 13 cm) long, and 1 to 2 inches (2.5 to 5 cm) wide. They can also be purchased canned in whole or diced form. Use Anaheim peppers in salsas, such as Salsa Roja Tatemada (page 41) and Salsa Verde (page 45), and dishes like Lentejas con Chile y Queso (page 90).

### Jalapeño

Jalapeño peppers are bright green, spicy, and 2 to 3 inches (5 to 7.5 cm) long. They are available canned, pickled, whole, and sliced. They make excellent salsas, like Salsa Jalapeño (page 31) and Salsa Fresca (page 39), and are great with fish (Pez Espada con Salsa Casera, page 159) or stuffed with cheese (Jalapeños Rellenos, page 68). When jalapeños are dried and smoked, they are called chipotle peppers. These smoky peppers can be purchased canned in an adobo sauce and make an excellent Salsa Chipotle (page 30) or Crema Chipotle (page 46). When cooking with chipotles, you can freeze extra chiles for later use. Place them on a parchment paper–lined baking sheet along with a little bit of the adobo sauce. Freeze and then remove from the baking sheet and place in a freezer bag.

### Pasilla

Pasilla peppers, otherwise known as *chiles negros*, are dried peppers usually used in combination with other peppers, such as ancho. They are mild in heat with a slightly pungent flavor.

### Poblano (ancho)

Poblano peppers are bright green in color and mild in flavor. They are 3 to 5 inches (7.5 to 13 cm) long and 2 to 3 inches (5 to 7.5 cm) wide. Use poblano chiles in Curtido de Elote con Chile Poblano (page 52) and Arroz con Crema y Chile Poblano (page 216). When dried, poblanos are referred to as ancho chiles and can be purchased whole or in powdered form. Use them in my Enchiladas de Pollo en Salsa de Chile Ancho recipe (page 176).

### Serrano

Serrano peppers are bright green and spicy. They can be 1 to 3 inches (2.5 to 7.5 cm) long and about ½ inch (13 mm) wide. Serranos are delicious when added to Mexican pinto beans, salsas like Salsa Roja Tatemada (page 41), and salads such as Ensalada de Coditos con Cilantro (page 125) and Ensalada de Atún en Aguacate (page 137).

## Especias Mexicanas
# MEXICAN SPICE BLEND
### ← · Makes 1 cup (240 ml · →

*Many savory recipes for Mexican cooking call for a combination of three items: garlic, peppercorns, and cumin seeds. The garlic and spices are the very essence of Mexico in a variety of dishes. In the southwestern United States, we are fortunate to have access to a store-bought Mexican spice mix that contains cumin seeds and peppercorns already blended. They are combined with fresh garlic and added to a molcajete, a lava rock mortar and pestle, and ground to a paste. This is the traditional way to prepare Mexican spices.*

*There are, however, different ways to prepare them. This blender version is easy to prepare and freeze for later use. Fresh garlic can then be added when preparing the recipe.*

**1 tablespoon plus 1 teaspoon cumin seeds**

**2 teaspoons black peppercorns**

**1.** Combine the spices in a blender with 1 cup (240 ml) water. Blend until the spices are almost completely pulverized. Spice particles may settle to the bottom. If this happens, shake or stir before using.

**2.** Use immediately or freeze in an ice cube tray or similar container for later use (see Note).

**NOTE:** *To make spice cubes, add the spice blend to small silicone molds or ice cube trays. Freeze; remove the frozen cubes from the molds and add to an airtight freezer bag; and then place the bag in another airtight freezer bag or container. The fragrance of these spices is very strong and will permeate other foods in your freezer if they aren't stored properly.*

––––––

1 recipe:
CALORIES 51; FAT 0 g (sat 0 g); PROTEIN 0.5 g; CARB 3 g; FIBER 1 g;
SUGARS 0 g (added sugars 0 g); SODIUM 2 mg

Salsa Chipotle
**CHIPOTLE SALSA**
30

Salsa Jalapeño
**JALAPEÑO SALSA**
31

Salsa Ranchera
**RANCHERO SAUCE**
33

**PICO DE GALLO**
34

Salsa de Chile Colorado
**RED CHILE SAUCE**
36

Salsa de Chile Colorado Bajo Calorías
**LIGHT RED CHILE SAUCE**
37

Salsa de Chile Ancho
**ANCHO CHILE SAUCE**
38

Salsa Fresca
**FRESH TOMATO SALSA**
39

Salsa Roja Tatemada
**ROASTED TOMATO SALSA**
41

Salsa de Tomatillo Sencilla
**SIMPLE TOMATILLO SAUCE**
42

Salsa de Tomatillo Tatemado
**ROASTED TOMATILLO SAUCE**
44

Salsa Verde
**GREEN SAUCE**
45

Crema Chipotle
**CHIPOTLE CREAM SAUCE**
46

Crema de Aguacate
**CREAMY AVOCADO SAUCE**
47

Guacamole con Comino Tostado
**GUACAMOLE WITH TOASTED CUMIN**
49

Curtido de Elote
**CORN RELISH**
50

Curtido de Cebolla y Tomate
**ONION AND TOMATO RELISH**
51

Curtido de Elote con Chile Poblano
**POBLANO CORN RELISH**
52

Dip con Frijol Negro y Elote
**BLACK BEAN AND
CORN DIP WITH CILANTRO**
54

Dip de Frijol con Chile California
**GREEN CHILE BEAN DIP**
55

Dip de Fiesta del Sol
**FIESTA DEL SOL DIP**
56

Dip de Yogurt con Salsa
**ZESTY YOGURT SALSA DIP**
57

SALSAS Y DIPS

# SALSAS & DIPS

Fresh salsas are amazing. They can change a dish from average to sublime. They are colorful, healthy, and full of nutrients. They have the ability to add flavor and fun to a simple meal. There are over fifty varieties of chiles that can be combined to make so many combinations of salsas—some mild, some hot. Perhaps my favorite of all salsas is the Salsa Ranchera (page 33), a family favorite. It's mild and ever so versatile.

This chapter also includes sauces that can be used to prepare various Mexican dishes, such as enchiladas; relishes, which pair well with many Mexican meals; and dips, which are perfect paired with a big bowl of baked chips (Tortillas Doradas, page 107) or vegetables.

Salsa Chipotle

# CHIPOTLE SALSA

**Makes 1½ cups (360 ml)**

*Chipotle peppers are actually smoked jalapeños in a red adobo sauce. They make a wonderful spicy salsa. This salsa adds smoky flavor to meats such as chicken or beef. Serve this with Quesadillas de Chile (page 66).*

One 8-ounce (227 g) can no-salt-added tomato sauce

3 chipotle peppers in adobo, with sauce

½ small onion, minced

1 garlic clove, minced

**1.** Combine the ingredients in a blender or food processor and blend until smooth.

**2.** Transfer the sauce to a skillet and simmer gently for about 10 minutes, until the flavors have blended well.

———

Per serving (2 tablespoons):
CALORIES 10; FAT 0 g (sat 0 g); PROTEIN 0.5 g; CARB 2 g; FIBER 0.5 g;
SUGARS 1 g; SODIUM 17 mg

Salsa Jalapeño

# JALAPEÑO SALSA

### ◂• Makes about 2 cups (550 g) •▸

*If you love jalapeños, you will love this sauce. It's so easy to prepare and amazing with tostadas. It can be served warm or cold—but it is picante (spicy)!*

1 tablespoon olive oil

1 small onion, chopped

1 garlic clove, minced

One 14.5-ounce (411 g) can no-salt-added diced tomatoes

½ cup (50 g) sliced pickled jalapeños, chopped

¼ teaspoon dried Mexican oregano

¼ teaspoon salt

**1.** Heat the oil in a nonstick skillet over medium heat and sauté the onion until translucent, 5 to 6 minutes. Add the garlic and sauté for about 1 minute more.

**2.** Add the tomatoes and their juices and stir to combine, then add the jalapeños, oregano, and salt.

**3.** Bring to a boil, then lower the heat and simmer for 15 to 20 minutes, stirring frequently, until the flavors have blended.

———

Per serving (¼ cup/69 g):
CALORIES 30; FAT 2 g (sat 0 g); PROTEIN 0.5 g; CARB 3.5 g; FIBER 1 g;
SUGARS 2 g; SODIUM 185 mg

## Salsa Ranchera
# RANCHERO SAUCE
**← · Makes about 9 cups (2.2 L) · →**

*This might be the most versatile Mexican sauce ever. The recipe was given to me by my in-laws and is a family favorite. Because it's so mild, it makes a great topping for meats, eggs, and tamales and a great dip for chips. It can also be used as a base to poach eggs or fish such as tilapia, or as a sauce over Huevos Rancheros Horneados (page 196). This cherished family recipe makes a large batch, and it freezes well.*

1 tablespoon olive oil

1 green bell pepper, seeded and finely chopped

1 onion, finely chopped

3 garlic cloves, minced

One 28-ounce (794 g) can diced tomatoes

One 28-ounce (794 g) can no-salt-added diced tomatoes

¼ cup (60 ml) Mexican Spice Blend (Especias Mexicanas, page 24)

1 cup (40 g) chopped cilantro

1 teaspoon salt

**1.** Heat the oil in a large pot or Dutch oven over medium heat and sauté the pepper and onion for about 5 minutes, or until the onion is translucent Add the garlic and sauté for 1 more minute. Add the tomatoes and their juices and stir to combine.

**2.** Add the spice blend to the pot, then add the cilantro and salt and bring to a boil. Reduce the heat, cover, and simmer on low for 60 to 90 minutes, until the sauce has thickened slightly and the flavors have blended.

———

Per serving (½ cup/120 ml):
CALORIES 32; FAT 1 g (sat 0 g); PROTEIN 1 g; CARB 5.5 g; FIBER 2 g;
SUGARS 3 g; SODIUM 221 mg

# PICO DE GALLO

### ← Makes 3 cups (515 g) →

*Pico de gallo is low in sodium, with a bright, vibrant flavor from the fresh lime juice. It can be eaten on its own or used to top nachos, enchiladas, and tacos. It goes especially well with Ensalada de Pollo (page 136). Add diced avocado and serve it with Tortillas Doradas (page 107) as a dip. If you have leftover pico de gallo, sauté it and scramble with eggs. It will keep for about two days in the refrigerator but is best if used fresh.*

3 medium tomatoes, seeded and chopped

½ small onion, chopped

⅔ cup (25 g) chopped cilantro

¼ cup (60 ml) fresh lime juice

1 fresh jalapeño or serrano chile, chopped (optional)

Combine all the ingredients in a medium bowl. Refrigerate for at least 2 hours and serve.

———

Per serving (½ cup/86 g):
CALORIES 20; FAT 0 g (sat 0 g); PROTEIN 1 g; CARB 4.5 g; FIBER 1 g;
SUGARS 2.5 g; SODIUM 8 mg

· · · · · · · · · · · · · · · · · · · · · · · · · **HEALTHY EASY MEXICAN** · · · · · · · · · · · · · · · · · · · · · · · · ·

34

## Salsa de Chile Colorado
# RED CHILE SAUCE
### ←· Makes about 3 cups (720 ml) ·→

*This basic chile sauce can be used for enchiladas, such as Enchiladas de Chile Colorado (page 199). Try adding it to a can of warmed, drained hominy with some diced pickled jalapenos. Serve warm topped with grated reduced-fat cheese. For a lower-calorie option, try the fat-free version of this recipe on page 37.*

¼ cup (60 ml) olive or canola oil

¼ cup plus 2 tablespoons (45 g) all-purpose flour

3 tablespoons chili powder, or to taste

1 garlic clove, minced

¼ cup (60 ml) Mexican Spice Blend (Especias Mexicanas, page 24)

½ teaspoon salt

**1.** Mix the oil and flour in a large nonstick skillet to make a paste. Allow to brown slowly over medium heat, stirring frequently, until it turns a sandy brown color, 5 to 10 minutes. Do not allow to smoke. Add the chili powder, stir well, and remove from the heat.

**2.** Slowly whisk in 2¾ cups (660 ml) water to form a smooth sauce, then return the skillet to the heat.

**3.** Add the garlic, spice blend, and salt to the sauce, then simmer for at least 10 minutes to allow the flavors to meld and the liquid to reduce a little. Cool slightly before using, as the sauce will thicken.

———

Per serving (¼ cup/60 ml):
CALORIES 65; FAT 5 g (sat 0 g); PROTEIN 1 g; CARB 4 g; FIBER 1 g;
SUGARS 0 g; SODIUM 116 mg

## Salsa de Chile Colorado Bajo Calorías
# LIGHT RED CHILE SAUCE
### ←·• Makes 2 cups (480 ml) •·→

*A special family recipe, this reduced-calorie version of Salsa de Chile Colorado (page 36) is great paired with Enchiladas de Hongo y Queso (page 202). It requires no oil to prepare, and the use of spices gives this sauce depth and character.*

¼ cup (30 g) all-purpose flour

2 teaspoons chili powder, or to taste

½ teaspoon black pepper

½ teaspoon ground cumin

½ teaspoon garlic powder

½ teaspoon onion powder

½ teaspoon salt

Pinch of paprika

**1.** Pour the flour into a large nonstick skillet. Over medium heat, slowly brown the flour, stirring often to prevent burning, for 11 to 12 minutes, until fragrant and pale brown in color. Watch carefully to prevent scorching.

**2.** Remove from the heat, then add the chili powder and stir to combine.

**3.** Return the pan to the heat and gradually whisk in 2 cups (480 ml) water until smooth. Add the remaining spices. Bring to a boil, then reduce the heat and simmer for 8 to 10 minutes to allow the flavors to blend.

———

Per serving (¼ cup/60 ml):
CALORIES 18; FAT 0 g (sat 0 g); PROTEIN 0.5 g; CARB 3.5 g; FIBER 0.5 g;
SUGARS 0 g; SODIUM 152 mg

## Salsa de Chile Ancho
# ANCHO CHILE SAUCE

**━· Makes about 2½ cups (600 ml) ·━**

*There are numerous ways to prepare this special salsa. This is by far the simplest method. You can also boil the ancho chiles and blend them with the other ingredients.*

6 or 7 dried red ancho chiles, stemmed with seeds removed

2 cups (480 ml) warm water

2 teaspoons tomato sauce

1½ teaspoons salt

2 garlic cloves

**1.** Place the chiles in a small bowl; cover with the warm water and allow to soften for about 5 minutes.

**2.** Transfer the chiles and water to a blender, then add the tomato sauce, salt, and garlic and blend until smooth.

**3.** Pass the sauce through a colander into a medium saucepan, pressing with the back of a spoon to separate small seeds and larger pieces that have not blended. Add a little water to the blender to get all of the sauce out.

**4.** Place the saucepan over low heat and simmer for 10 to 15 minutes, to desired consistency.

―――――

Per serving (¼ cup/60 ml):
CALORIES 35; FAT 1 g (sat 0 g); PROTEIN 1.5 g; CARB 61 g; FIBER 2.5 g;
SUGARS 0 g; SODIUM 360 mg

## Salsa Fresca
# FRESH TOMATO SALSA
#### ←· **Makes about 4 cups (960 ml)** ·→

*This sauce is easy to make, because you simply put all the ingredients into a blender. It can be frozen for several months or kept for four to five days in the refrigerator. It's especially good served slightly warm, served over Tortas (page 205).*

4 medium tomatoes, quartered

½ cup (60 g) chopped onion

1 jalapeño, seeded and chopped

3 garlic cloves, minced

½ cup (20 g) chopped cilantro

2 tablespoons fresh lime juice

Combine all the ingredients in a blender or food processor and blend until your desired consistency is achieved.

———

Per serving (½ cup/120 ml):
CALORIES 23; FAT 0 g (sat 0 g); PROTEIN 1 g; CARB 5 g; FIBER 1 g;
SUGARS 2.5 g; SODIUM 12 mg

## Salsa Roja Tatemada
# ROASTED TOMATO SALSA

**➛• Makes about 3 cups (720 ml) •➛**

*Roasting tomatoes and chiles over a mesquite fire makes the flavor of this salsa even better! This salsa can be eaten warm or cold. Serve it over Tacos de Puerco Pernil en Olla de Cocción Lenta (page 149) and add Crema Chipotle (page 46) for a special treat. When making salsas, I like to start with a smaller amount of chile and add more if needed.*

4 medium tomatoes, halved and seeded

½ onion, separated into layers

2 serrano chiles, or to taste

1 garlic clove

½ teaspoon salt

Chopped cilantro (optional)

**1.** Place the tomatoes, onion, chiles, and garlic in a large, dry, heavy skillet and "roast" over medium heat until well charred, but not burned, for 25 to 30 minutes. Turn frequently to achieve an even char.

**2.** Transfer to a blender with ½ cup (120 ml) water. Cover, remove the blender lid's center insert, and cover the opening with a clean kitchen towel. Blend to your desired consistency.

**3.** Transfer to a saucepan and simmer for 10 to 15 minutes, until your desired consistency is achieved. Add cilantro, if desired.

**4.** Cool slightly and refrigerate for 3 to 4 hours to allow the flavors to blend, then serve.

———

Per serving (¼ cup/60 ml):
CALORIES 11; FAT 0 g (sat 0 g); PROTEIN 0.5 g; CARB 2.5 g; FIBER 0.5 g;
SUGARS 1.5 g; SODIUM 101 mg

## Salsa de Tomatillo Sencilla
# SIMPLE TOMATILLO SAUCE
### ←· Makes 2½ cups (360 ml) ·→

*Tomatillos are small, tart fruits with a papery husk that should be removed before cooking. Look for fresh tomatillos with husks that have a vibrant green color and fresh husk. Rich in vitamins A and C and antioxidants, they can be combined with other ingredients to make great Mexican sauces. This is the perfect sauce for Enchiladas Suizas (page 174). For a smokier variation, try my Salsa de Tomatillo Tatemado (page 41), in which the tomatillos are pan-roasted instead of boiled.*

1½ pounds (680 g) tomatillos, husked and rinsed to remove stickiness

2 tablespoons olive oil

½ onion, chopped

2 garlic cloves, minced

Salt

Black pepper

**1.** Bring a large pot of water to a boil and add the tomatillos. Allow them to boil until they sink to the bottom and turn an olive-green color, 10 to 15 minutes. Do not allow them to burst. Remove from the water and transfer to a blender.

**2.** Heat the oil in a skillet over medium heat. Add the onion and sauté until translucent, 5 to 6 minutes. Add the garlic and sauté for 1 minute more. Remove from the heat.

**3.** Transfer the onion and garlic to the blender. Remove the blender lid's center insert, and cover with a clean kitchen towel. Blend until smooth. Season with salt and pepper.

———

Per serving (¼ cup/60 ml, without salt):
CALORIES 49; FAT 3.5 g (sat 0 g); PROTEIN 1 g; CARB 5 g; FIBER 1.5 g;
SUGARS 0 g; SODIUM 1 mg

## Salsa de Tomatillo Tatemado
# ROASTED TOMATILLO SAUCE
#### ⤙· Makes 2 cups (480 ml) ·⤚

*This is one of the most delicious salsas you will ever eat. It takes a little bit of time to prepare, but the steps are easy, and the flavor is out-of-this-world good! If the salsa is too tart, add a bit of sugar to balance the flavor.*

1 pound (455 g) tomatillos (about 12 medium), husked and rinsed to remove stickiness

½ onion, separated into layers

1 jalapeño, stemmed

2 garlic cloves, minced

½ cup (20 g) chopped cilantro

¾ teaspoon salt

½ teaspoon black pepper

**1.** Place the tomatillos, onion, jalapeño, and garlic in a large, dry, heavy skillet over medium-high heat. Allow to char slowly, but not burn, turning frequently to allow all sides to cook, 25 to 30 minutes. Remove from the heat.

**2.** Transfer to a blender with the cilantro, salt, and pepper. Remove the blender lid's center insert and cover with a clean kitchen towel. Blend until slightly chunky.

**3.** Transfer to a saucepan and heat for 10 to 15 minutes to allow the flavors to blend.

———

Per serving (½ cup/120 ml):
CALORIES 47; FAT 1 g (sat 0 g); PROTEIN 1.5 g; CARB 9 g; FIBER 3 g;
SUGARS 1 g; SODIUM 440 mg

· · · · · · · · · · · · · · · · · · · · · · · · · **HEALTHY EASY MEXICAN** · · · · · · · · · · · · · · · · · · · · · · · · ·

44

## Salsa Verde
# GREEN SAUCE
### ←· Makes 5 cups (1.2 L) ·→

*This sauce makes a great enchilada sauce, but it can also be spooned over grilled chicken or fish. Combining tomatillos and spinach makes this salsa rich in vitamins A, C, and K. The addition of corn tortillas gives this sauce a unique corn flavor.*

1 fresh Anaheim chile

10 ounces (285 g) tomatillos (about 7 to 10 medium), husked and rinsed to remove stickiness

¼ cup (30 g) chopped onion

3 corn tortillas (Tortillas de Maíz, page 105), torn into small pieces

3 garlic cloves

4 ounces (115 g) fresh spinach, chopped (about 3 cups)

3 cups (720 ml) low-sodium chicken or vegetable broth

½ teaspoon salt

**1.** Place the chile on a hot griddle or skillet over medium-high heat and roast until thoroughly blistered and charred on all sides, about 15 minutes, turning frequently. Transfer to a clean damp kitchen towel and let cool. Carefully peel off the charred skin and remove the veins and seeds, then set aside.

**2.** In a large saucepan filled with water, boil the tomatillos for 5 to 10 minutes, until they turn olive green and sink to the bottom. Remove from the heat and drain.

**3.** Transfer the tomatillos to a blender or food processor, then add all the other ingredients and blend until smooth. Remove the blender lid's center insert and cover with a clean kitchen cloth while blending.

**4.** Return the mixture to the saucepan. Cover, bring to a boil, then reduce the heat and simmer for 60 minutes to allow the flavors to blend.

———

Per serving (½ cup/120 ml):
CALORIES 36; FAT 1 g (sat 0 g); PROTEIN 1 g; CARB 6 g; FIBER 1 g;
SUGARS 0.5 g; SODIUM 219 mg

### Crema Chipotle

# CHIPOTLE CREAM SAUCE

**← · Makes ½ cup (120 g) · →**

*This sauce is typically made with Mexican crema, which tastes like a combination of sour cream and crème fraîche. Crema is often used as a garnish in Mexican dishes. This recipe calls for reduced-fat sour cream, cutting the calories but keeping the taste! You'll absolutely love this sauce on Tacos de Pavo con Frijoles y Chile (page 186) or Pollo Rancho King (page 172). If you like the sauce thinner, add a little more skim milk.*

½ cup (120 g) reduced-fat sour cream

2 teaspoons skim milk

2 tablespoons finely chopped cilantro

1 chipotle chile, finely chopped, plus adobo sauce, to taste

⅛ teaspoon salt

2 tablespoons fresh lime juice

Combine the ingredients in a small mixing bowl and mix well. Refrigerate for 1 to 2 hours to allow the flavors to blend.

———

Per serving (2 tablespoons):
CALORIES 52; FAT 4 g (sat 2 g); PROTEIN 5.5 g; CARB 8 g; FIBER 0 g;
SUGARS 2.5 g; SODIUM 102 mg

## Crema de Aguacate
# CREAMY AVOCADO SAUCE
### ← · Makes about 3½ cups (840 ml) · →

*Adding heart-healthy avocados to Greek yogurt makes a creamy, good-for-you sauce that is great as a dip as well as a topping for Nachos con Frijoles, Queso y Aguacate (page 62). I also love using this sauce with Tacos de Pescado con Ensalada de Repollo (page 157). If you like your sauce a little thinner, use skim milk to thin it out a bit.*

2 avocados, peeled and pitted

1 cup plus 2½ tablespoons (285 g) low-fat plain
  Greek yogurt

¼ cup (60 ml) fresh lime juice

¼ cup (10 g) chopped cilantro

1 garlic clove, minced

½ teaspoon salt

Place all the ingredients in a blender container and blend until smooth, about 5 minutes. Refrigerate for at least 2 hours to allow flavors to blend.

————

Per serving (2 tablespoons):
CALORIES 30; FAT 2 g (sat 0.5 g); PROTEIN 1 g; CARB 1.5 g; FIBER 1 g;
SUGARS 0.5 g; SODIUM 47 mg

Guacamole con Comino Tostado

# GUACAMOLE WITH TOASTED CUMIN

### ◄· Makes about 2½ cups (530 g) ·►

*Toasting cumin seeds gives this guacamole a unique flavor. The lime juice adds brightness, and the vegetables add a nice texture. Try this for a different twist to guacamole, served with Tortillas Doradas (page 107)! Avocados not ripe? Place them in a brown paper bag with an apple and store for a few days. If you don't use the whole avocado, squeeze a little lemon or lime juice on the cut side and cover tightly with plastic wrap to keep it fresh.*

½ teaspoon cumin seeds

2 large avocados, peeled and pitted

⅛ teaspoon salt

Black pepper, to taste

1 Roma tomato, chopped

2 scallions, finely chopped

2 tablespoons chopped cilantro

2 tablespoons fresh lime juice

**1.** Place the cumin seeds in a small dry skillet over medium heat and toast for about 1 minute, until fragrant. Transfer to a molcajete or a spice grinder and grind to a paste. Set aside.

**2.** Place the avocados in a medium bowl and mash roughly. Add the salt, pepper, and ground cumin seeds and stir to combine.

**3.** Mix in the tomato, scallions, cilantro, and lime juice. Refrigerate to allow the flavors to blend. Serve chilled.

———

Per serving (¼ cup/53 g):
CALORIES 65; FAT 6 g (sat 1 g); PROTEIN 1 g; CARB 3 g; FIBER 2 g;
SUGARS 0.5 g; SODIUM 33 mg

## Curtido de Elote
# CORN RELISH
### ←·• Makes 3 cups (715 g) •·→

*This relish can be used as a dip with chips, or as a garnish alongside chicken or beef fajitas. Serve it as an accompaniment to Tacos de Pavo con Crema Chipotle (page 185) or Tacos de Pescado con Ensalada de Repollo (page 157). It looks pretty plated with other Mexican foods and is a great way to incorporate more vegetables in your diet.*

¼ cup (50 g) sugar

1 teaspoon ground turmeric

¾ teaspoon ground celery seed

¼ cup (60 ml) white vinegar

1 tablespoon cornstarch

2 cups (270 g) frozen corn kernels, thawed and pan-roasted, or kernels from 4 ears fresh corn, pan-roasted

¼ cup (30 g) chopped red onion

1 small tomato, seeded and diced

2 tablespoons chopped green bell pepper

2 tablespoons chopped cilantro

**1.** Combine the sugar, turmeric, celery seed, and vinegar in a microwave-safe bowl. Microwave on high for about 1½ minutes, until thoroughly warmed.

**2.** Combine the cornstarch and ¼ cup (60 ml) water in a small bowl and mix thoroughly to form a slurry.

**3.** Whisk the cornstarch slurry into the warmed vinegar mixture. Microwave for about 1 minute, until the mixture begins to bubble and thicken.

**4.** Add the corn, onion, tomato, pepper, and cilantro and mix well. Refrigerate for at least 2 hours and serve cold.

———

Per serving (½ cup/119 g):
CALORIES 86; FAT 0.5 g (sat 0 g); PROTEIN 2 g; CARB 21 g; FIBER 2 g;
SUGARS 10 g; SODIUM 4 mg

## Curtido de Cebolla y Tomate
# ONION AND TOMATO RELISH

**← · Makes 2½ cups (500 g) · →**

*My father-in-law made this simple salsa to be served with breakfast tacos. It's delicious, especially with Chorizo de Pavo (page 188). The vinegar enhances the flavor of the fresh tomatoes.*

3 medium tomatoes (about 1 pound/455 g), seeded
    and diced

1 small sweet onion, chopped

¼ cup (60 ml) red wine vinegar

½ teaspoon salt

¼ teaspoon black pepper

Toss together all the ingredients in a medium bowl.

———

Per serving (½ cup/100 g):
CALORIES 26; FAT 0.5 g (sat 0 g); PROTEIN 1 g; CARB 6 g; FIBER 1 g;
SUGARS 4 g; SODIUM 241 mg

## Curtido de Elote con Chile Poblano
# POBLANO CORN RELISH
### ⤚· Makes 2½ cups (435 g) ·⤙

*This corn relish is made with roasted poblano chiles, milder chiles that add spice and flavor.*

2 fresh poblano chiles

1½ tablespoons olive oil

1 small onion, diced

1 garlic clove, minced

2 cups (270 g) frozen corn kernels, thawed, or kernels
   from 3 fresh ears of corn

2 tablespoons chopped cilantro

¼ teaspoon salt

¼ teaspoon black pepper

**1.** Preheat the oven to 425°F (220°C). Line a baking sheet with foil.

**2.** Place the chiles on the baking sheet. Brush lightly with ½ tablespoon of the oil and roast for 20 to 30 minutes, turning occasionally, until the skin has completely blistered. Immediately wrap the chiles in a clean damp kitchen towel and set aside.

**3.** Pour the remaining 1 tablespoon oil into a medium skillet over medium heat. Sauté the onion until translucent, 5 to 6 minutes. Add the garlic and sauté for 1 minute longer. Add the corn and cook for about 10 minutes.

**4.** Meanwhile, remove the chiles from the towel. Peel off and discard the charred skin. Remove the stems and seeds, then chop the chiles into small pieces.

**5.** Add the chiles, cilantro, salt, and pepper to the corn mixture and continue to cook for about 5 minutes more, until heated through. Serve warm.

———

Per serving (½ cup/110 g):
CALORIES 95; FAT 5 g (sat 0 g); PROTEIN 2 g; CARB 14 g; FIBER 2 g;
SUGARS 2.5 g; SODIUM 119 mg

· · · · · · · · · · · · · · · · · · · · · · · · · **HEALTHY EASY MEXICAN** · · · · · · · · · · · · · · · · · · · · · · · ·

52

# BLACK BEAN AND CORN DIP WITH CILANTRO

**←· Makes about 4½ cups (1.3 kg) ·→**

*The beans and corn in this wonderful dip add lots of fiber and color to the dish. The addition of lime juice and fresh cilantro gives it a fresh, vibrant taste. This dip is easy to put together when friends drop by. Serve with Tortillas Doradas (page 107).*

One 15-ounce (425 g) can black beans, rinsed and drained

One 15-ounce (425 g) can white corn, drained

1½ cups (360 ml) mild picante sauce, such as Pace

½ cup (20 g) chopped cilantro

¼ cup (60 ml) fresh lime juice

Mix all the ingredients together in a medium bowl.

———

Per serving (½ cup/145 g):
CALORIES 67; FAT 1 g (sat 0 g); PROTEIN 17 g; CARB 15 g; FIBER 3 g;
SUGARS 1.5 g; SODIUM 649 mg

· · · · · · · · · · · · · · · · · · · · · · · · ·· **HEALTHY EASY MEXICAN** · · · · · · · · · · · · · · · · · · · · · · · · ·

54

## Dip de Frijol con Chile California
# GREEN CHILE BEAN DIP

**← · Makes about 3 cups (640 g) · →**

*This easy dip can be made with leftover pinto beans. You can easily adjust the heat by adding more hot sauce or a different type of chile.*

2 cups (340 g) drained cooked pinto beans

½ cup (120 g) drained canned diced green chiles

½ cup (120 ml) no-salt-added tomato sauce

⅓ cup (40 g) chopped onion

1 tablespoon apple cider vinegar

5 dashes hot sauce, such as Tabasco

**1.** Place all the ingredients in a food processor or blender and blend until smooth.

**2.** Refrigerate for 4 to 5 hours or overnight to allow the flavors to blend, then warm in a saucepan over low heat before serving.

———

Per serving (½ cup/106 g):
CALORIES 92; FAT 0 g (sat 0 g); PROTEIN 5 g; CARB 17 g; FIBER 6 g;
SUGARS 3 g; SODIUM 64 mg

## Dip de Fiesta del Sol
# FIESTA DEL SOL DIP
**← · Makes about 3½ cups (755 g) · →**

*This dip can be served with Tortillas Doradas (page 107) or baked pita chips. Because it's made with cottage cheese, it's a good source of calcium!*

2 cups (450 g) 1 percent small-curd cottage cheese

2 Roma tomatoes, seeded and diced

½ cup (120 g) drained canned diced green chiles

½ cup (50 g) chopped scallions

½ teaspoon salt

½ teaspoon Worcestershire sauce

3 dashes hot sauce, such as Tabasco

**1.** Place the ingredients in a blender or food processor and blend until smooth.

**2.** Refrigerate for about 4 hours or overnight to allow the flavors to blend, then serve cold.

———

Per serving (½ cup/107 g):
CALORIES 56; FAT 1 g (sat 0.5 g); PROTEIN 8 g; CARB 4 g; FIBER 1 g;
SUGARS 3 g; SODIUM 484 mg

## Dip de Yogurt con Salsa
# ZESTY YOGURT SALSA DIP
**━·• Makes about 2½ cups (720 g) •·━**

*Greek yogurt has a tart, rich taste. When combined with a prepared salsa and fresh vegetables, it makes a great dip that is rich in protein and calcium. It tastes good, too! You can add cilantro, tomatoes, and green chiles to make it even more interesting.*

2 cups (490 g) low-fat plain Greek yogurt

¾ cup (180 ml) Ranchero Sauce (Salsa Ranchera, page 33) or prepared salsa

½ cup (50 g) chopped scallions

Mix all the ingredients together in a medium bowl. Refrigerate for at least 6 hours or overnight, then serve.

———

Per serving (⅓ cup/90 g):
CALORIES 55; FAT 1.5 g (sat 1 g); PROTEIN 6 g; CARB 4 g; FIBER 1 g;
SUGARS 2 g; SODIUM 64 mg

## APERITIVOS ~ APPETIZERS

Nachos con Frijoles, Queso y Aguacate
### BEAN, CHEESE, AND AVOCADO NACHOS 62

Hongos con Queso y Chile Verde
### STUFFED MUSHROOMS WITH GREEN CHILE CREAM CHEESE 63

Quesadillas a la Parrilla
### GRILLED QUESADILLAS WITH SCALLIONS AND LIME 65

Quesadillas de Chile
### CHILE QUESADILLAS 66

Jícama con Chile y Lima
### CHILE-LIME JICAMA 67

Jalapeños Rellenos
### CHEESY STUFFED JALAPEÑOS 68

## ACOMPAÑAMIENTOS ~ SIDES

Calabacitas
### MEXICAN SQUASH 70

Posole Blanco con Hongos y Queso
### HOMINY AND CHEESE CASSEROLE 71

Ejotes Guisados
### MEXICAN-STYLE GREEN BEANS 73

Elote Mexicano
### MEXICAN CORN 74

Posole Mexicano
### MEXICAN HOMINY 75

Calabaza Sur Tejano
### SOUTH TEXAS SQUASH CASSEROLE 76

Calabaza y Elote con Queso
### CHEESY ZUCCHINI WITH CORN 78

Espinacas Mexicanas
### MEXICAN-STYLE SPINACH 79

# APERITIVOS Y ACOMPAÑAMIENTOS

# APPETIZERS & SIDES

**M**ake appetizers fun! Usually, I like to keep them on the lighter side when they accompany Mexican mains, to provide just a little introduction to what's to come. These recipes contain simple, fresh ingredients, making them healthy as well as delicious. For a cheesy appetizer, try my Quesadillas a la Parilla (page 65) or Jalapeños Rellenos (page 68), or start your meal with fresh Jícama con Chile y Lima (page 67). You'll have so much fun cooking these appetizers and even more fun eating them!

My plant-based sides are perfect served with any main—plant-based or otherwise. Pair my Calabacitas (page 70), Ejotes Guisados (page 73), or Espinacas Mexicanas (page 79) with any entrée for a complete, nutritious meal.

## Nachos con Frijoles, Queso y Aguacate

# BEAN, CHEESE, AND AVOCADO NACHOS

**⤙· Serves 6 ·⤚**

*This recipe is proof that the whole family can enjoy eating healthy food that is fun and delicious. These nachos are just as satisfying as regular nachos, but so much better for you. Sometimes, I add leftover shredded grilled chicken breast for even more flavor.*

Nonstick cooking spray

30 baked tortilla chips (Tortillas Doradas, page 107)

3 cups (510 g) cooked pinto beans, mashed and warmed slightly

6 ounces (170 g) reduced-fat mozzarella or Monterey Jack, grated (1½ cups)

3 Roma tomatoes, seeded and diced

½ cup (120 g) drained canned diced green chiles or pickled jalapeños

1 large avocado, peeled, pitted, and diced

**1.** Preheat the oven to 350°F (180°C). Spray a baking sheet with cooking spray.

**2.** Spread the tortilla chips on the baking sheet. Top with the beans, then sprinkle with the cheese, tomatoes, and chiles.

**3.** Bake for 5 to 10 minutes, until the cheese is melted. Just before serving, add the avocado.

———

Per serving:
CALORIES 293; FAT 12 g (sat 1 g); PROTEIN 16 g; CARB 36 g; FIBER 11 g; SUGARS 4 g; SODIUM 329 mg

## Hongos con Queso y Chile Verde

# STUFFED MUSHROOMS WITH GREEN CHILE CREAM CHEESE

**← · Serves 6 · →**

*Green chiles are mild, and, when combined with cheese, they add a little zest to your mushrooms. You can add a little hot sauce for even more flavor.*

Nonstick cooking spray

12 large white mushrooms

4 tablespoons butter/oil blend, such as Land O'Lakes butter with olive oil

½ cup (80 g) finely chopped onion

¼ cup (60 g) drained canned diced green chiles

¼ cup (60 g) neufchatel cream cheese

½ teaspoon salt

¼ teaspoon black pepper

**1.** Preheat the oven to 350°F (180°C). Spray a baking sheet with cooking spray.

**2.** Separate the mushroom stems from the caps, then finely chop the stems.

**3.** Heat 2 tablespoons of the butter in a nonstick skillet over medium heat and sauté the mushroom stems and onion until the onion is translucent, 3 to 5 minutes. Add the chiles and warm through for 1 to 2 minutes.

**4.** Transfer to a bowl, then mix in the cream cheese, salt, and pepper. Set aside.

**5.** Heat the remaining 2 tablespoons butter in the skillet over medium heat. Sauté the mushrooms caps until they are tender but still retain their shape, 5 to 10 minutes. Remove from the heat and let cool slightly.

**6.** Stuff the mushroom caps with the cream cheese mixture. Place on the baking sheet and bake for 5 to 10 minutes to warm through. Serve immediately.

———

Per serving:
CALORIES 104; FAT 9 g (sat 4 g); PROTEIN 3 g; CARB 4 g; FIBER 1 g; SUGARS 2 g; SODIUM 327 mg

## Quesadillas a la Parrilla

# GRILLED QUESADILLAS WITH SCALLIONS AND LIME

**←· Serves 4 ·→**

*These quesadillas are so simple—they make a great light appetizer before a big meal. The lime juice adds a fresh citrus zing.*

4 corn tortillas (Tortillas de Maíz, page 105)

4 ounces (115 g) part-skim mozzarella, grated (1 cup)

½ cup (50 g) chopped scallions

3 tablespoons fresh lime juice

**1.** Place the tortillas on a heated grill or dry skillet over medium heat to warm slightly, 30 to 60 seconds, then flip and warm on the other side.

**2.** Scatter the cheese and scallions over the tortillas, then sprinkle with the lime juice.

**3.** Continue to warm the quesadillas until the cheese has melted, 3 to 4 minutes. Fold each tortilla in half and serve.

———

Per serving:
CALORIES 136; FAT 6 g (sat 3 g); PROTEIN 10 g; CARB 13 g; FIBER 2 g;
SUGARS 2 g; SODIUM 283 mg

## Quesadillas de Chile
# CHILE QUESADILLAS
### ← · Serves 4 · →

*Quesadillas are such a versatile Mexican dish. They can be served for breakfast, lunch, or dinner, with hundreds of different fillings. Serve these with a warm smoky salsa, such as Salsa de Tomatillo Tatemado (page 44), for a great breakfast.*

8 corn tortillas (Tortillas de Maíz, page 105)

8 ounces (225 g) reduced-fat Monterey Jack, grated (2 cups)

½ cup (120 g) drained canned diced green chiles

**1.** Thoroughly warm the tortillas on a heated griddle or dry skillet over medium heat for 2 to 3 minutes on each side.

**2.** Sprinkle the cheese and chiles on each tortilla, fold in half, and continue warming until the cheese melts, 3 to 4 minutes.

———

Per serving:
CALORIES 260; FAT 13 g (sat 8 g); PROTEIN 17 g; CARB 22 g; FIBER 3 g;
SUGARS 0 g; SODIUM 824 mg

## Jícama con Chile y Lima
# CHILE-LIME JICAMA

**←· Serves 6 ·→**

*Jicama is a low-calorie vegetable that is crisp and delicious. It's wonderful served as a light appetizer or snack. The chili powder and lime juice give it a spark.*

1 medium jicama, peeled and sliced into thin wedges

⅓ cup (80 ml) fresh lime juice

2 teaspoons chili powder

½ teaspoon salt

**1.** Place the jicama wedges in a large mixing bowl. Add the lime juice and gently toss to combine. Set aside.

**2.** Mix together the chili powder and salt in a small bowl.

**3.** Dip the inner edge of each wedge into the chili-salt mixture and arrange on a platter. Serve chilled.

———

Per serving:
CALORIES 48; FAT 0 g (sat 0 g); PROTEIN 1 g; CARB 11 g; FIBER 6 g;
SUGARS 3 g; SODIUM 207 mg

## Jalapeños Rellenos
# CHEESY STUFFED JALAPEÑOS
**Serves 6**

*These are great football-watching appetizers. The cheese tones down the heat from the jalapeños.*

Nonstick cooking spray

⅓ cup (85 g) neufchatel cream cheese

2 ounces (55 g) reduced-fat sharp cheddar, finely grated (½ cup)

¼ cup (25 g) chopped scallions

12 whole pickled jalapeños, halved lengthwise, seeds and membranes removed

**1.** Preheat the oven to 350°F (180°C). Spray a baking sheet with cooking spray.

**2.** Mix the cheeses and scallions in a medium bowl.

**3.** Use a small spoon to stuff each jalapeño half with the cheese mixture, then place on the prepared baking sheet. Bake for about 10 minutes, until the cheeses have melted slightly, then serve.

---

Per serving:
CALORIES 72; FAT 5 g (sat 3 g); PROTEIN 4 g; CARB 1 g; FIBER 0 g;
SUGARS 0 g; SODIUM 521 mg

## Calabacitas
# MEXICAN SQUASH
### ➤· Serves 6 ·➤

*Two different types of squash are made more flavorful in this recipe with onions, peppers, and cilantro. Serve with Carne Guisada (page 144).*

1 tablespoon olive oil

½ cup (80 g) finely chopped onion

½ red bell pepper, chopped

2 medium zucchini, julienned

2 medium yellow squash, julienned

½ teaspoon minced garlic

½ teaspoon salt

⅛ teaspoon chili powder

1 tablespoon finely chopped cilantro

**1.** Heat the oil in a large skillet over medium heat. Gently sauté the onion and pepper until tender, about 5 minutes. Add the garlic and sauté for 1 more minute, until fragrant.

**2.** Add the squash and sauté for 5 to 7 minutes, until cooked but still a little firm.

**3.** Toss the squash with the salt and chili powder, then top with the cilantro and serve immediately.

––––––––

Per serving:
CALORIES 51; FAT 3 g (sat 0 g); PROTEIN 2 g; CARB 7 g; FIBER 2 g;
SUGARS 4 g; SODIUM 198 mg

## Posole Blanco con Hongos y Queso
# HOMINY AND CHEESE CASSEROLE

➼ **· Serves 6 ·** ➼

*This dish is a great accompaniment to Pollo Adobado (page 171). It's also a delicious meatless meal on its own. Try making this using garbanzo beans for a filling meal. The diced jalapeños add a nice little kick!*

One 15.5-ounce (439 g) can hominy, drained and rinsed

One 10.5-ounce (298 g) can reduced-fat cream of mushroom soup

1 jalapeño, seeded and diced

4 ounces (115 g) reduced-fat cheddar, grated (1 cup)

**1.** Preheat the oven to 350°F (180°C).

**2.** Heat the hominy in a medium saucepan over medium heat until thoroughly warmed, 7 to 10 minutes. Pour out any liquid, then add the mushroom soup and jalapeño and cook for an additional 5 minutes, or until heated through.

**3.** Transfer to a shallow baking dish. Top with the cheese, then bake for 5 minutes, to allow the cheese to melt.

———

Per serving:
CALORIES 120; FAT 5 g (sat 3 g); PROTEIN 6 g; CARB 10 g; FIBER 1 g;
SUGARS 1 g; SODIUM 573 mg

Ejotes Guisados

# MEXICAN-STYLE GREEN BEANS

← · Serves 4 · →

*This dish can be prepared in one skillet. Add cubes of panela cheese to make a complete meal, or serve with Pollo en Salsa Naranja en Olla de Cocción Lenta (page 169).*

1 tablespoon olive or canola oil

½ cup (60 g) chopped onion

2 garlic cloves, minced

One 16-ounce (454 g) package frozen green beans

One 14.5-ounce (411 g) can no-salt-added diced tomatoes, drained

½ teaspoon salt

Black pepper, to taste

**1.** Heat the oil in a large skillet over medium heat. Sauté the onion until translucent, 5 to 6 minutes. Add the garlic and sauté 1 minute.

**2.** Add the green beans, tomatoes, salt, and pepper. Simmer for 15 minutes, stirring often, until heated through.

———

Per serving:<br>
CALORIES 127; FAT 4 g (sat 0 g); PROTEIN 3 g; CARB 15 g; FIBER 6 g;<br>
SUGARS 9 g; SODIUM 322 mg

## Elote Mexicano
# MEXICAN CORN
### ⤙ · Serves 4 · ⤚

*This is a colorful and tasty corn dish. Add diced jalapeños or charred poblanos for even more flavor and spice.*

1 tablespoon olive oil

½ cup (60 g) chopped onion

2 cups (270 g) frozen corn kernels, thawed

2 tablespoons pimientos

**1.** Heat the oil in a large nonstick skillet over medium heat. Sauté the onion until tender, 5 to 6 minutes. Remove from the pan.

**2.** Sauté the corn and pimientos until the corn is slightly browned. Add the onion and heat thoroughly, 3 to 4 minutes more. Serve warm.

———

Per serving:
CALORIES 96; FAT 4 g (sat 0 g); PROTEIN 2 g; CARB 16 g; FIBER 2 g;
SUGARS 2 g; SODIUM 3 mg

Posole Mexicano
# MEXICAN HOMINY
#### ➤· Serves 6 ·➤

*Hominy is corn that has been dried and processed. Corn was first domesticated by the indigenous people of Mexico over ten thousand years ago, and it remains an essential ingredient in Mexican cooking to this day.*

1 tablespoon olive oil

¾ cup (90 g) chopped onion

One 15.5-ounce (439 g) can golden hominy, drained

1¼ cups (300 g) canned no-salt-added crushed tomatoes

1 cup (240 ml) Red Chile Sauce (Salsa de Chile Colorado, page 36)

1 cup (115 g) shredded reduced-fat Mexican-style cheese blend

**1.** Heat the oil in a large nonstick skillet over medium heat. Sauté the onion until tender, 5 to 6 minutes. Add the hominy and tomatoes and stir to combine. Heat for 5 minutes.

**2.** Add the sauce and heat thoroughly. Pour into a casserole dish and sprinkle with the cheese. Serve immediately.

———

Per serving:
CALORIES 151; FAT 7 g (sat 1 g); PROTEIN 8 g; CARB 15 g; FIBER 4 g;
SUGARS 3 g; SODIUM 328 mg

## Calabaza Sur Tejano
# SOUTH TEXAS SQUASH CASSEROLE
### ←· Serves 8 ·→

*Mixing beautiful yellow squash with onions and tomatoes makes this dish colorful as well as nutritious.*

Nonstick cooking spray

1 tablespoon olive or canola oil

1 cup (120 g) chopped onion

6 medium yellow squash, thinly sliced

½ cup (120 g) canned diced tomatoes and green chiles (such as Ro-Tel)

⅛ teaspoon black pepper, or to taste

4 ounces (115 g) part-skim mozzarella, grated (1 cup)

**1.** Preheat the oven to 350°F (180°C). Spray a medium baking dish with cooking spray.

**2.** Heat the oil in a large skillet over medium heat. Add the onion and sauté until translucent, 5 to 6 minutes. Add the squash and continue to sauté, tossing gently, until cooked through and still somewhat firm, 4 to 5 minutes.

**3.** Transfer to the baking dish. Add the tomatoes and pepper and stir to combine.

**4.** Bake for 20 minutes, then remove from the oven and top with the cheese. Bake for 10 minutes, or until bubbly.

———

Per serving:
CALORIES 88; FAT 5 g (sat 0 g); PROTEIN 6 g; CARB 9 g; FIBER 3 g; SUGARS 5 g; SODIUM 102 mg

## Calabaza y Elote con Queso
# CHEESY ZUCCHINI WITH CORN
**Serves 6**

*Just a small amount of reduced-fat cream cheese gives this dish a creamy taste without too many calories or saturated fat.*

1 tablespoon olive or canola oil

¼ cup (25 g) chopped scallions

1 garlic clove, minced

6 medium zucchini, thinly sliced

2 cups (270 g) frozen corn kernels, thawed

¼ cup (60 ml) low-sodium chicken broth

4 ounces (115 g) neufchatel cream cheese

2 tablespoons 2 percent milk

⅛ teaspoon salt

⅛ teaspoon black pepper

**1.** Heat the oil in a large nonstick skillet over medium heat. Sauté the scallions until translucent, 5 to 6 minutes. Add the garlic and sauté for 1 more minute, until fragrant.

**2.** Add the zucchini and sauté until cooked through but still firm, about 8 minutes. Mix in the corn and toss gently until heated through, 4 to 5 minutes.

**3.** Add the broth and simmer gently for 2 to 3 minutes.

**4.** Mix the cheese, milk, salt, and pepper in a medium bowl until smooth. Add to the pan, warm through, and serve immediately.

———

Per serving:
CALORIES 148; FAT 7 g (sat 3 g); PROTEIN 6 g; CARB 18 g; FIBER 5 g; SUGARS 12 g; SODIUM 155 mg

## Espinacas Mexicanas
# MEXICAN-STYLE SPINACH
#### ← · Serves 4 · →

*Spinach is considered a superfood because it contains vitamins A, C, and K, as well as folate, potassium, calcium, and fiber. Serve with quesadillas for a simple, delicious meal.*

10 ounces (285 g) baby spinach

1½ teaspoons olive oil

1 small onion, finely chopped

2 garlic cloves, minced

2 medium tomatoes, seeded and chopped

½ teaspoon salt

⅛ teaspoon black pepper

**1.** Bring a large pot of water to a boil. Blanch the spinach until wilted, about 1 minute. Drain in a colander, let cool, and gently squeeze out all of the water. Set aside.

**2.** Heat the oil in a large skillet over medium heat. Sauté the onion until translucent, 5 to 6 minutes. Add the garlic and sauté for 1 more minute, until fragrant.

**3.** Add the tomatoes and cook, stirring frequently, until the tomatoes have softened, about 5 minutes. Add the spinach and warm through. Season with the salt and pepper.

――――――

Per serving:
CALORIES 66; FAT 2 g (sat 0 g); PROTEIN 3 g; CARB 12 g; FIBER 4 g;
SUGARS 3 g; SODIUM 410 mg

· · · · · · · · · · · · · · · · · · · · · · · · · · **APPETIZERS & SIDES** · · · · · · · · · · · · · · · · · · · · · · · · · ·

79

## CALDOS Y SOPAS
## SOUPS

Caldo de Res con Papas, Elote y Calabaza
### BEEF SOUP WITH POTATOES, CORN, AND ZUCCHINI
84

Sopa de Albóndigas
### MEXICAN TURKEY MEATBALL SOUP
85

Lentejas Mexicanas
### MEXICAN LENTIL SOUP
87

Caldo Tlalpeño
### TLALPEÑO SOUP
89

Lentejas con Chile y Queso
### LENTILS WITH GREEN CHILES AND CHEESE
90

Caldo de Mariscos
### MEXICAN SEAFOOD SOUP
91

Caldo de Pollo con Tallarines
### MEXICAN CHICKEN NOODLE SOUP
92

Sopa de Tortilla
### TORTILLA SOUP
94

Sopa de Tomatillo y Maíz
### TOMATILLO CORN SOUP
96

## PANES
## BREADS

Semita de Anís
### MEXICAN ANISE BREAD
99

Bolillos
### MEXICAN ROLLS
101

Pan de Campo
### COWBOY BREAD
103

Tortillas de Maíz
### CORN TORTILLAS
105

Tortillas Doradas
### BAKED TORTILLA CHIPS
107

Tortillas para Tacos
### TACO SHELLS
108

Tortillas de Harina
### FLOUR TORTILLAS
109

Tortillas de Trigo Integral
### WHOLE WHEAT TORTILLAS
110

CALDOS, SOPAS
Y PANES

# SOUPS & BREADS

There's nothing more delicious than a bowl of steaming soup, loaded with vegetables and accompanied by freshly made corn tortillas (Tortillas de Maíz, page 105). I like making large batches of soups and keeping them in the freezer for a quick meal. Soups can be filling and rich in nutrients.

As we're being encouraged to move more toward plant-based meals, the humble lentil is coming to the forefront as a tiny nutrition powerhouse. When prepared in soups, salads, or side dishes, lentils can make an extraordinary and economical meal.

Corn and flour tortillas have always been mainstays of Mexican cooking. I learned to make tortillas from my mother. It takes a little bit of practice to make these delectable treats perfectly round! We always laughed at the unusual shapes that I created on my quest for the perfect tortilla!

Here, I've taken decades-old recipes for breads and tortillas and adapted them to use vegetable oils instead of the traditional animal fats. Some of my recipes for breads and tortillas have been made healthier by incorporating whole grains. Taking these small steps in our kitchens can mean a lifetime of better health.

## Caldo de Res con Papas, Elote y Calabaza
# BEEF SOUP WITH POTATOES, CORN, AND ZUCCHINI

**━·Serves 4·━**

*This soup is flavorful and hearty. It's loaded with vitamins A and C from the carrots and cabbage. The corn and zucchini add additional fiber and vitamins, too. It's best served with warm, freshly made corn tortillas (Tortillas de Maíz, page 105).*

1 tablespoon olive oil

1 pound (455 g) very lean round steak, excess fat removed, cut into 1-inch (2.5 cm) cubes

2 carrots, peeled and cut into 1-inch (2.5 cm) slices

2 ears fresh corn, cut into 4-inch (10 cm) pieces

2 medium zucchini, cut into thick rounds

2 medium russet potatoes, quartered

½ head green cabbage, quartered

½ onion, sliced

¼ green bell pepper, sliced

2 garlic cloves, crushed

½ cup (120 ml) Mexican Spice Blend (Especias Mexicanas, page 24)

½ cup (120 ml) no-salt-added tomato sauce

1 teaspoon salt (optional)

Black pepper, to taste (optional)

¼ cup (10 g) chopped cilantro

**1.** Heat the oil in a large pot over medium heat. Sauté the beef until well browned, 5 to 10 minutes. Drain any excess fat.

**2.** Add 7 cups (1.7 L) water and bring to a boil. Reduce the heat, then add the carrots, corn, zucchini, potatoes, cabbage, onion, bell pepper, garlic, spice blend, and tomato sauce. Add the salt and black pepper, if desired.

**3.** Bring to a boil. Reduce the heat to low, cover, and simmer gently for 45 minutes, until the flavors have blended. Add the cilantro and simmer for 15 minutes more.

———

Per serving (without salt):
CALORIES 321; FAT 11 g (sat 3 g); PROTEIN 31 g; CARB 25 g; FIBER 7 g;
SUGARS 10 g; SODIUM 102 mg

# Sopa de Albóndigas

# MEXICAN TURKEY MEATBALL SOUP

**━•· Serves 8 ·•━**

*Albóndigas is Spanish for "little meatballs." These are healthier than regular beef meatballs, because they are prepared with ground turkey breast, which is lower in saturated fat and a leaner source of protein. This soup is excellent served with homemade corn tortillas (Tortillas de Maíz; page 105). It also freezes well.*

**MEATBALLS**

1 pound (455 g) ground turkey breast

4 ounces (115 g) reduced-fat pork sausage

½ cup (90 g) cooked brown or white rice

¼ cup (30 g) all-purpose flour

1 teaspoon ground cumin

**SOUP**

1 tablespoon olive oil

1 large onion, chopped

1½ teaspoons ground cumin

3 garlic cloves, minced

One 14-ounce (397 g) can petite diced tomatoes

10 cups (2.4 L) low-sodium beef broth

2 cups fresh (310 g) or frozen (270 g) corn kernels, no salt added

½ cup (20 g) chopped cilantro

Lime wedges

**1.** Preheat the oven to 450°F (230°C). Line a baking sheet with parchment paper.

**2.** To make the meatballs, combine the turkey, sausage, rice, flour, cumin, and ¼ cup (60 ml) water in a large bowl. Shape into meatballs about 1½ inches (4 cm) in size and place on the prepared baking sheet.

**3.** Bake for 30 minutes, or until browned, turning occasionally to allow for even browning. Drain excess fat and set aside.

**4.** To make the soup, heat the oil in a large pot over medium heat. Sauté the onion and cumin for about 5 minutes, until translucent. Add the garlic and sauté for 1 additional minute.

**5.** Add the tomatoes and their juices. Add the broth, corn, and meatballs, then cover and simmer for 30 minutes, until the flavors have blended.

**6.** Top with the cilantro and serve with lime wedges.

———

Per serving:
CALORIES 196; FAT 6 g (sat 1 g); PROTEIN 21 g; CARB 16 g; FIBER 2 g;
SUGARS 5 g; SODIUM 439 mg

### Lentejas Mexicanas

# MEXICAN LENTIL SOUP

**➤· Serves 4 ·➤**

*Lentils are a good source of protein, fiber, calcium, and iron. When combined with corn tortillas (Tortillas de Maíz, page 105), lentils make a complete protein and a great meatless meal.*

1 tablespoon olive oil

1 carrot, peeled and chopped

1 celery rib, chopped

1 small onion, chopped

1 cup (180 g) brown lentils, rinsed, picked through, and drained

¼ cup (60 ml) dry red wine

1½ teaspoons chili powder

1 bay leaf

½ teaspoon salt

¼ teaspoon black pepper

½ teaspoon ground cumin

1 medium tomato, seeded and chopped

2 scallions, thinly sliced diagonally (optional)

**1.** Heat the oil in a Dutch oven or large pot over medium heat. Sauté the carrot, celery, and onion until tender, 5 to 6 minutes.

**2.** Add the lentils and wine and bring to a boil. Cook over medium-high heat until the liquid is almost evaporated.

**3.** Stir in 3½ cups (840 ml) water and the spices and bring to a boil. Decrease the heat to low, cover, and simmer for 30 minutes, or until the lentils are tender.

**4.** Stir in the tomato and cook for 15 minutes more. Remove the bay leaf; top with the scallions, if desired; and serve.

---

Per serving:
CALORIES 220; FAT 4 g (sat 0 g); PROTEIN 14 g; CARB 32 g; FIBER 15 g;
SUGARS 6 g; SODIUM 329 mg

# Caldo Tlalpeño
# TLALPEÑO SOUP
## ➤· Serves 8 ·➤

*The name of this soup comes from the Tlalpan area of Mexico City, where it originated. It's not your usual chicken soup—it's served with chunks of fresh avocado and rice on the side. The addition of avocado tempers the wonderful smoky flavor and heat that the chipotle adds.*

8 cups (2 L) reduced-sodium chicken broth

1½ pounds (680 g) chicken breast meat, sliced about 2½ inches (6.5 cm) wide and 2 inches (5 cm) thick

1 tablespoon olive or canola oil

1 onion, diced

2 carrots, peeled and thinly sliced

1 celery rib, finely chopped

1 medium zucchini, finely chopped

¼ cup (60 ml) Mexican Spice Blend (Especias Mexicanas, page 24)

2 tablespoons tomato sauce

1 chipotle pepper in adobo, sliced (or more, to taste)

½ teaspoon black pepper

4 cups (740 g) cooked brown or white rice

1 avocado, peeled, pitted, and chopped

Lime wedges

**1.** Bring the chicken broth to a boil in a Dutch oven or large pot. Add the chicken, bring to a boil again, cover, and simmer for 15 to 20 minutes, until the meat is no longer pink. Remove the chicken from the broth and shred using two forks. Skim any foam from the top of the broth.

**2.** Heat the oil in a large nonstick skillet over medium heat. Sauté the onion until translucent, 5 to 6 minutes. Add the carrots, celery, and zucchini and sauté until tender, 5 to 6 minutes.

**3.** Transfer the sautéed vegetables to the pot with the chicken broth and add the spice blend, tomato sauce, chipotle, and black pepper. Cover and simmer gently for 15 to 20 minutes, until the flavors have blended.

**4.** Serve with the rice, avocado, and lime wedges on the side.

———

Per serving:
CALORIES 290; FAT 9 g (sat 1 g); PROTEIN 24 g; CARB 28 g; FIBER 4 g;
SUGARS 3 g; SODIUM 189 mg

## Lentejas con Chile y Queso
# LENTILS WITH GREEN CHILES AND CHEESE

➤· **Serves 5** ·➤

*This rich lentil chili features Anaheim chile and Monterey Jack cheese. Lentils are an inexpensive way to incorporate protein, fiber, and iron into your diet.*

1 Anaheim chile

1 teaspoon olive oil

½ cup (50 g) minced scallions

2 garlic cloves, minced

One 14-ounce (397 g) can no-salt-added diced tomatoes

2 carrots, peeled and thinly sliced

¾ cup (135 g) brown lentils

½ teaspoon chili powder

½ teaspoon salt

3¼ cups (780 g) low-sodium beef or vegetable broth

¼ cup (28 g) grated reduced-fat Monterey Jack

**1.** Preheat oven to 425°F (220°C). Line a baking sheet with foil.

**2.** Place the chile on the baking sheet and flatten gently. Brush lightly with oil. Roast for about 20 minutes, turning occasionally to ensure even cooking, until the skin has completely blistered.

**3.** Remove from the oven and place in a clean kitchen towel. Set aside for about 10 minutes. Once the chile has cooled, peel the charred skin. Chop and set aside.

**4.** Combine the scallions, garlic, and tomatoes with their juices in a large pot over medium high heat, stirring often. Add the chile, carrots, lentils, chili powder, salt, and broth and bring to a boil.

**5.** Cover, reduce the heat, and simmer for about 30 minutes, until the lentils are tender. Serve topped with the cheese.

———

Per serving (without tortillas):
CALORIES 158; FAT 3 g (sat 1 g); PROTEIN 12 g; CARB 24 g; FIBER 11 g;
SUGARS 6 g; SODIUM 419 mg

# Caldo de Mariscos
# MEXICAN SEAFOOD SOUP
### ➤· Serves 4 ·➤

*Caldo de Mariscos is a popular soup in South Texas. Different types of fish and sometimes shrimp are added to the soup for variation. Adding vegetables makes it rich in vitamin C as well as fiber.*

1 tablespoon olive oil

1 cup (120 g) chopped onion

2 medium tomatoes, seeded and chopped

2 medium zucchini, chopped

¼ cup (40 g) diced green bell pepper

3 garlic cloves, crushed

½ teaspoon ground cumin

¼ cup (10 g) chopped cilantro

¼ cup (60 ml) fresh lime juice

2 tablespoons Mexican Spice Blend (Especias Mexicanas, page 24)

2 bay leaves

1 teaspoon dried Mexican oregano, or to taste

½ teaspoon salt

2 pounds (910 g) snapper fillets, cut into 2-inch (5 cm) pieces

Corn tortillas (Tortillas de Maíz, page 105)

**1.** Heat the oil in a Dutch oven or large pot over medium heat. Sauté the onion until translucent, 5 to 6 minutes. Add the tomatoes, zucchini, and pepper and sauté until tender, about 5 minutes. Add the garlic and cumin and cook for about 1 more minute.

**2.** Add the cilantro, lime juice, spice blend, bay leaves, oregano, and salt along with 4 cups (960 ml) water and bring to a boil. Cover, lower the heat, and simmer for about 40 minutes, stirring occasionally, to allow the flavors to blend. Add the fish during the last 10 minutes of cooking, cover again, and cook through.

**3.** Remove the bay leaves and serve with warm corn tortillas.

––––––––

Per serving (without tortillas):
CALORIES 309; FAT 7 g (sat 1 g); PROTEIN 49 g; CARB 11 g; FIBER 3 g;
SUGARS 6 g; SODIUM 448 mg

# Caldo de Pollo con Tallarines
# MEXICAN CHICKEN NOODLE SOUP

**←·· Serves 6 ··→**

*My grandmother used to make homemade noodles for her chicken soup. These noodles are thick and wonderful. They make this nourishing soup a true comfort food. You can increase the nutritional value by adding sliced zucchini.*

**SOUP**

1½ pounds (680 g) chicken breast meat, sliced into 2-inch (5 cm) cubes

One 14-ounce (340 g) can no-salt-added crushed tomatoes

2 cups (340 g) baby carrots

½ onion, cut into thin wedges

¼ cup (35 g) roughly chopped green bell pepper

2 garlic cloves, minced

½ cup (120 ml) Mexican Spice Blend (Especias Mexicanas, page 24)

1½ teaspoons salt

1 bay leaf

½ cup (20 g) chopped cilantro

**NOODLES**

1½ cups (180 g) all-purpose flour

½ teaspoon salt

2 tablespoons fresh lime juice, or to taste

Corn tortillas (Tortillas de Maíz, page 105)

**1.** To make the soup, place the chicken in a Dutch oven or large pot with 8 cups (2 L) water and the bay leaf. Cook over medium-high heat until the chicken is tender, 7 to 10 minutes, or until the internal temperature reaches 160°F (70°C). Remove the chicken from the broth, then skim any foam from the top of the broth.

**2.** Add the tomatoes, carrots, onion, pepper, garlic, spice blend, salt, and bay leaf to the broth. Bring to a boil; reduce the heat to low and simmer, covered, for about 20 minutes.

**3.** While the soup is simmering, prepare the noodles. Whisk together the flour and salt in a large bowl. Add about ½ cup (120 ml) water and mix with your hands. Knead slightly to form a dough ball. Place the dough on a lightly floured work surface and roll out into an oblong shape, about ¼ inch (6 mm) thick.

**4.** Cut the dough into noodles about ½ inch (12 mm) wide. Add to the simmering soup and cook for about 15 minutes, until the noodles are tender.

**5.** Return the chicken to the soup and simmer briefly to warm through. Drizzle the lime juice over the soup and serve with corn tortillas.

––––––

Per serving (without tortillas):
CALORIES 288; FAT 2 g (sat 0 g); PROTEIN 31 g; CARB 34 g; FIBER 4 g;
SUGARS 6 g; SODIUM 878 mg

## Sopa de Tortilla
# TORTILLA SOUP
**➳· Serves 4 ·➳**

Tortilla soup is so named for the strips of tortillas that are placed in the bowl and on top of the soup as a garnish. This recipe is simple. You can add other vegetables, such as zucchini or corn, to make it more nourishing. You can also use leftover chicken to make preparation supereasy. This is a great soup to keep in the freezer.

2 medium tomatoes, halved

1 tablespoon olive or canola oil

1 cup (140 g) finely chopped onion

2 garlic cloves, minced

1 pound (455 g) chicken breast meat, cooked and shredded

4 cups (960 ml) low-sodium chicken broth

½ teaspoon black pepper

¼ cup (10 g) chopped cilantro

4 corn tortillas (Tortillas de Maíz, page 105), cut into strips and baked (see Note)

**1.** Char the tomatoes in a dry skillet over medium-high heat for 15 to 25 minutes; turn frequently, allowing all sides to char evenly.

**2.** While the tomatoes cook, heat the oil in a Dutch oven or large pot over medium heat and sauté the onion until translucent, 5 to 6 minutes. Add the garlic and sauté for 1 minute, until fragrant.

**3.** Transfer the tomatoes, onion, and garlic to a blender or food processor and blend until smooth. If the tomatoes are still hot, remove the blender lid's center insert before blending and cover with a clean kitchen towel to allow the steam to vent.

**4.** Pour the vegetable mixture back into the pot, then add the chicken, chicken broth, and pepper and bring to a boil. Cover, reduce the heat, and simmer for 20 minutes to allow the flavors to blend. Add the cilantro and continue to simmer for 10 more minutes. Serve immediately, topped with the tortilla strips.

*Note: Sopa de Tortilla is typically served with lots of fried tortilla chips in the soup. Since this recipe is prepared with baked chips, it's best to serve them on top, as a garnish. Place the tortilla strips in a single layer on a baking sheet and bake at 400°F (200°C) for 3 to 4 minutes, then flip them over and bake about 3 more minutes, making sure they don't burn.*

———

Per serving:
CALORIES 252; FAT 7 g (sat 0 g); PROTEIN 30 g; CARB 18 g; FIBER 3 g;
SUGARS 4 g; SODIUM 306 mg

## Sopa de Tomatillo y Maíz

# TOMATILLO CORN SOUP

➤· **Serves 4** ·➤

*I once tasted a delightful soup at a restaurant on the San Antonio River Walk. It was spicy yet tart, with delicious corn undertones. It inspired me to develop a recipe that tasted exactly like the original!*

1 pound (455 g) tomatillos, husked and rinsed to remove stickiness

1 tablespoon olive or canola oil

¼ onion, chopped

2 garlic cloves, minced

2 corn tortillas (Tortillas de Maíz, page 105), chopped

2 cups (480 ml) low-sodium chicken broth

½ teaspoon ground cumin

½ teaspoon salt

½ cup (20 g) chopped cilantro (optional)

½ cup (60 g) roasted pepitas (optional)

½ cup (120 g) reduced-fat sour cream (optional)

**1.** Bring a large pot of water to a boil and add the tomatillos. Boil until the tomatillos turn olive green and float to the top, 10 to 15 minutes. Drain and transfer to a blender.

**2.** While the tomatillos are cooking, heat the oil in a skillet over medium heat and sauté the onion until translucent, 5 to 6 minutes. Add the garlic and sauté until fragrant, 1 more minute.

**3.** Transfer the onion and garlic to the blender along with the tortillas, broth, cumin, and salt. Carefully blend until smooth. If the tomatillos are still hot, remove the blender lid's center insert before blending and place a clean kitchen towel over the opening.

**4.** Transfer the tomatillo mixture to a medium saucepan and gently simmer for 15 to 20 minutes to allow the flavors to blend.

**5.** Serve with the cilantro, pepitas, and sour cream, if desired.

———

Per serving (without cilantro, pepitas, or sour cream):
CALORIES 107; FAT 6 g (sat 0 g); PROTEIN 3 g; CARB 14 g; FIBER 3 g;
SUGARS 0 g; SODIUM 407 mg

### Semita de Anís

# MEXICAN ANISE BREAD

**⤙· Makes 12 rolls ·⤚**

*Aniseed has a wonderful licorice flavor and is used often in Mexican baked goods. This semita is excellent as a breakfast bread, dessert, or merienda, the Mexican tradition of having a midafternoon coffee or tea with a pastry. You can add golden raisins to the dough before kneading for an even more delicious bread.*

4½ to 5 cups (540 to 600 g) all-purpose flour, plus more for dusting

¼ cup (50 g) sugar

One ¼-ounce (7 g) packet active dry yeast

1 teaspoon salt

1 cup (240 ml) anise tea (see Note), unstrained, cooled to lukewarm

2 eggs

¼ cup (60 ml) canola oil, plus more to coat the bowl

2 tablespoons aniseed

**1.** Sift together 2 cups (240 g) of the flour, the sugar, yeast, and salt in a large bowl. Add the anise tea along with its seeds, then use an electric mixer to mix for 1 minute at slow speed. Add the eggs, oil, and aniseed and beat for 3 minutes at high speed, until blended.

**2.** Stir in the remaining flour, a little at a time, just until the dough comes together. Turn out onto a floured work surface and knead for 4 to 5 minutes, until the dough is smooth and elastic. Add more flour if needed.

**3.** Lightly coat a large bowl with oil, then add the dough. Turn the dough over to coat with oil. Cover the bowl with a damp cloth and let the dough rise in a warm place (100°F/40°C) for at least 1 hour, until doubled in size.

**4.** Divide the dough into twelve pieces, then form into small, smooth, dome-shaped mounds, about 4 inches (10 cm) in diameter. Line a baking sheet with parchment paper, then place the mounds on top.

**5.** Cover with a clean kitchen towel and allow the dough to rise in a proofing oven or warm, draft-free place (100°F/40°C) for 30 to 35 minutes, until doubled in size.

**6.** Preheat the oven to 375°F (190°C). Bake for 12 to 15 minutes, until golden brown. Remove from the oven and let cool on wire racks.

**Note:** *Prepare anise tea by boiling 2 teaspoons aniseed in 1½ cups (360 ml) water for 10 to 15 minutes, to your desired strength.*

———

Per serving (1 roll):
CALORIES 256; FAT 6 g (sat 1 g); PROTEIN 7 g; CARB 43 g; FIBER 2 g;
SUGARS 5 g; SODIUM 206 mg

### Bolillos

# MEXICAN ROLLS

### ━•· Makes 12 small rolls ·━

*Bolillos are small oblong loaves, similar to French bread. They're usually cut in half horizontally and filled with an array of fillings to make sandwiches called tortas. A bean and cheese bolillo (Tortas con Frijoles y Queso, page 205), served with Salsa Ranchera (page 33) or a similar salsa, is wonderful for breakfast or a light lunch.*

2 tablespoons butter/oil blend, such as Land O'Lakes butter with olive oil

1½ tablespoons sugar

2 teaspoons salt

One ¼-ounce (7 g) packet active dry yeast

5 to 5½ cups (600 to 660 g) all-purpose flour (or 2½ cups/300 g all-purpose flour and 2½ cups/ 380 g whole wheat flour), plus more for dusting

Canola or other vegetable oil, to grease the bowl

**1.** Gently heat the butter, sugar, salt, and 2 cups (480 g) water in a medium saucepan over low heat, bringing it to 115°F (45°C). Add the yeast and stir well to dissolve.

**2.** Transfer to a large bowl. Add 1 cup (120 g) of the flour and beat well with a fork. Gradually add the remaining flour, 1 cup (120 g) at a time, stirring well after each addition.

**3.** Turn the dough out onto a lightly floured work surface. Knead for 4 to 5 minutes, until the dough is smooth and elastic.

**4.** Lightly coat a large bowl with oil and place the dough inside, turning once to oil the top of the dough. Cover the bowl with a damp cloth and leave it in a warm place (100°F/40°C) to rise for 1 to 1½ hours, or until doubled in size.

**5.** Line two baking sheets with parchment paper. Gently punch down the dough and divide into twelve pieces. Shape into small oblong loaves about 5 inches (12.5 cm) long and tapered at the edges. Place on the prepared baking sheets.

**6.** Use a sharp razor blade to create a slit 3 inches (7.5 cm) long on top of each loaf. Let rise again in a warm place (100°F/40°C) for about 35 minutes, or until doubled in size.

**7.** Preheat the oven to 350°F (180°C).

**8.** Bake for 30 to 35 minutes, until golden brown. Remove from the oven and let cool on a wire rack before serving.

———

Per serving:
CALORIES 208; FAT 3 g (sat 1 g); PROTEIN 5 g; CARB 40 g; FIBER 1 g;
SUGARS 2 g; SODIUM 404 mg

## Pan de Campo
# COWBOY BREAD
### ⤙ · Serves 12 · ⤚

*My grandfather was a real-life Texas cowboy, a vaquero. While driving cattle through Texas, it was customary to bake* pan de campo *in a cast-iron skillet. The ingredients could be carried easily and made into a quick, tasty bread. This version is prepared with oil rather than shortening and is just as good!*

Nonstick cooking spray

2 cups (240 g) all-purpose flour (or 1 cup/120 g all-purpose flour and 1 cup/150 g whole wheat flour), plus more for dusting

2 teaspoons baking powder

1 teaspoon salt

½ teaspoon sugar

⅓ cup (80 ml) canola oil

⅔ cup (140 ml) 2 percent milk

**1.** Preheat the oven to 350°F (180°C). Spray a baking sheet with cooking spray.

**2.** Sift together the flour, baking powder, salt, and sugar in a large bowl, then add the oil. Use a pastry blender to form a crumbly mixture, then add the milk and work the dough until it forms a ball, 2 to 3 minutes. If the dough still feels sticky to the touch, add a little extra flour. Remove the dough from the bowl and knead until a smooth ball forms, about 1 minute.

**3.** Transfer to a lightly floured work surface and roll out into a circle about 11 inches (28 cm) in diameter and about ½ inch (13 mm) thick.

**4.** Place the dough on the prepared baking sheet. Bake for 25 to 30 minutes, until golden brown. Cut into 12 equal wedges and serve warm.

––––––––––

Per serving:
CALORIES 135; FAT 6 g (sat 1 g); PROTEIN 3 g; CARB 16 g; FIBER 1 g;
SUGARS 1 g; SODIUM 249 mg

## Tortillas de Maíz
# CORN TORTILLAS
### ←·  **Makes eighteen 5-inch (13 cm) tortillas**  ·→

*These are such a special treat and don't take very long to prepare. You need masa harina (flour made from nixtamalized corn), a tortilla press, and, preferably, a large electric griddle that heats to at least 400°F (200°C). A large griddle is best, because it heats more evenly and can cook more tortillas at a time. (If you don't have a large griddle, a good quality skillet that heats evenly will do.) These tortillas are wonderful with Caldo Tlalpeño (page 89) and Posole de Puerco y Pollo (page 147).*

> 2 cups (240 g) masa harina, such as Maseca
>
> 1 teaspoon salt (optional)
>
> 1½ cups (300 ml) lukewarm water, plus more as needed

**1.** Sift together the masa harina and salt, if using, into a large bowl. Add 1 cup (240 ml) of the lukewarm water and mix, using your hands. The dough should become moistened and start to come together.

**2.** Add the remaining water and work the dough by hand for 5 to 10 minutes, until there's no dough stuck to the sides of the bowl. The masa should feel smooth and slightly moist. If the dough seems dry, add a little more lukewarm water and continue kneading. If the dough sticks to your hand, it needs a little more kneading. If it no longer sticks to your hand, it's ready to shape.

**3.** Form a large dough ball, then divide into eighteen small, golf ball–size pieces and shape into balls. Return the dough balls to the bowl, cover with a clean damp kitchen towel, and let rest for about 15 minutes.

**4.** Heat an electric griddle to 400°F (200°C) or a skillet over medium-high heat for about 5 minutes.

**5.** Cut a piece of thick plastic wrap large enough to cover both sides of the tortilla press. The plastic should be folded in half with the folded edge placed against the hinge of the press.

**6.** Place a ball of dough in the center of the tortilla press between the two plastic-wrapped sides. Close the top of the press and press the lever down. The tortilla should be about ⅛-inch (3 mm) thick, about 5 inches (13 cm) in diameter. If the tortilla is too thin, it may break when you transfer it to the griddle. If it's too thick, it may not cook properly.

**7.** Cook the tortilla for about 2 minutes on one side, until the edges begin to lift slightly. Flip and cook on the other side for about 1 minute, until slight brown spots are visible. Repeat with the remaining dough balls until all the tortillas are pressed and cooked.

———

Per tortilla:
CALORIES 47; FAT 1 g (sat 0 g); PROTEIN 1 g; CARB 10 g; FIBER 1 g;
SUGARS 0 g; SODIUM 129 mg

## Tortillas Doradas
# BAKED TORTILLA CHIPS
**← · Serves 6 · →**

*These gluten-free baked chips are delicious as a base for healthy nachos (Nachos con Frijoles, Queso y Aguacate, page 62) or served with salsas or dips (such as Dip de Frijol Negro con Elote, page 54). They are also excellent with Sopa de Tortilla (page 94). Bake them whole to use them for Tostadas de Frijol y Queso (page 198).*

¼ teaspoon salt

⅛ teaspoon chili powder

6 corn tortillas (Tortillas de Maíz, page 105, or store-bought)

1 teaspoon olive oil

**1.** Preheat the oven to 400°F (200°C).

**2.** Mix the salt and chili powder in a small bowl.

**3.** Lightly brush both sides of the tortillas with the oil. Sprinkle lightly with the salt and chili mixture.

**4.** Use a sharp knife to cut each tortilla into 6 wedges. Place on a baking sheet.

**5.** Bake for 5 minutes, checking often to make sure the chips do not burn.

**6.** Remove from the oven and turn each chip over to allow for even baking. Return to the oven and bake for 3 to 4 minutes, until crisp. Serve warm or cold. Store in an airtight container for up to 1 week.

———

Per serving:
CALORIES 54; FAT 1.5 g (sat 0 g); PROTEIN 1 g; CARB 10 g; FIBER 1 g;
SUGARS 0 g; SODIUM 227 mg

Tortillas para Tacos

# TACO SHELLS

**◂· Makes 16 taco shells ·▸**

*Baked taco shells are lower in fat and calories than fried or store-bought taco shells. When you make them at home, the flavor is better, because your ingredients are fresh. These can be prepared ahead of time, if needed. Fill these baked taco shells with chicken, beef, or pork. Even though they take a little more time to prepare, they are worth it.*

Nonstick cooking spray

16 corn tortillas (Tortillas de Maíz, page 105, or store-bought)

**1.** Heat an electric griddle to 450°F (230°C) or a heavy skillet over medium-high heat.

**2.** Spray the griddle or skillet with cooking spray. Add a tortilla to the pan and cook for 2 to 3 minutes, until warmed. Flip the tortilla and gently fold in half. Cook for 1 to 2 minutes. Continue to flip the folded tortilla until it is golden brown and crispy. Remove from the griddle and repeat with the remaining tortillas, spraying the griddle as needed.

———

Per taco shell:
CALORIES 47; FAT 1 g (sat 0 g); PROTEIN 1 g; CARB 10 g; FIBER 1 g;
SUGARS 0 g; SODIUM 129 mg

## Tortillas de Harina
# FLOUR TORTILLAS
**←·· Makes eighteen 6-inch (15 cm) tortillas ··→**

*These tortillas are made healthier with oil instead of the traditional shortening or lard. You can use any oil you prefer; canola and olive oil are two good options. Homemade tortillas take just a few minutes to prepare and can be filled with meats, cheese, eggs, and even nut butters! They go especially well with Pollo Guisado (page 164) or Fideo con Pavo (page 189).*

3 cups (360 g) all-purpose flour, plus more for dusting

1 tablespoon baking powder

1 teaspoon salt

¼ cup (60 ml) canola oil

1 cup (240 ml) boiling water

**1.** Sift together the flour, baking powder, and salt in a large bowl. Add the oil and combine with a dough blender.

**2.** Slowly add the boiling water. Continue to blend with the dough blender until the dough is workable with your hands. Form a ball and knead on a floured work surface for 3 to 5 minutes, until the ball is smooth.

**3.** Place in a bowl, cover with a clean damp kitchen towel, and allow to rest for 20 minutes.

**4.** Heat an electric griddle to 400°F (200°C) or a heavy skillet over medium-high heat.

**5.** Divide the dough into eighteen pieces and form into balls. Lightly flour a work surface and your rolling pin. Roll each ball into a 6-inch (15 cm) circle about ⅛-inch (3 mm) thick.

**6.** Transfer to the hot griddle or skillet and cook for about 2 minutes, until small brown spots appear. Flip and cook for about 3 minutes on the other side. (Timing may vary according to the heating capabilities of your griddle or skillet.)

**7.** As the tortillas cook, keep them warm and pliable in an insulated tortilla warmer or clean kitchen towel.

———

Per tortilla:
CALORIES 100; FAT 3 g (sat 0 g); PROTEIN 2 g; CARB 15 g; FIBER 1 g;
SUGARS 0 g; SODIUM 196 mg

## Tortillas de Trigo Integral
# WHOLE WHEAT TORTILLAS
### ←· **Makes twelve 6-inch (15 cm) tortillas** ·→

*These tortillas, made with whole wheat flour and olive oil, are healthier than traditional flour tortillas made with all refined flour and shortening or lard. They make excellent breakfast tacos and quesadillas and can be filled with a variety of fillings. They are especially wonderful for Quesadillas de Chile (page 66). If you don't plan to cook them right away, it's best to roll out all of the tortillas at the same time and save them in between layers of wax paper. They will keep for two or three days in the refrigerator.*

1 cup (120 g) all-purpose flour, plus more
    for dusting

1 cup (150 g) whole wheat flour

2 teaspoons baking powder

¾ teaspoon salt

3 tablespoons olive oil

½ cup (120 ml) boiling water, plus more
    if needed

**1.** Sift the flours, baking powder, and salt together in a large bowl. Add the oil and use a pastry blender to mix it into the dry ingredients until a crumbly mixture forms, about 3 minutes.

**2.** Add the boiling water and blend with the pastry blender until cool enough to handle with your hands. Knead the dough until a smooth ball forms, about 5 minutes.

**4.** Cover the bowl with a clean damp kitchen towel and allow the dough to rest for 20 minutes.

**5.** Divide the dough evenly into twelve pieces and form into balls. Lightly flour a work surface and your rolling pin. Roll each ball out into a circle about 6 inches (15 cm) in diameter and ⅛ inch (3 mm) thick.

**6.** Heat an electric griddle to 400°F (200°C) or a heavy skillet over medium-high heat.

**7.** Place each tortilla on the hot griddle or skillet and cook for about 5 minutes, until small brown spots appear. Flip and cook for about 3 minutes on the other side. (Timing may vary according to the heating capabilities of your griddle or skillet.)

**6.** As the tortillas cook, keep them warm and pliable in an insulated tortilla warmer or clean kitchen towel.

---

Per tortilla:
CALORIES 109; FAT 4 g (sat 0 g); PROTEIN 3 g; CARB 17 g; FIBER 2 g;
SUGARS 0 g; SODIUM 213 mg

ENSALADAS

# SALADS

These wonderful salads will enhance any meal. Many of them can also be made into complete meals by adding a cooked lean meat. Keeping greens on hand in your refrigerator helps you throw together a simple salad at any time, or perhaps something more elaborate like the recipes in this chapter. I prefer organic greens that are prewashed and ready to be made into salads by adding simple ingredients such as mandarin oranges, apples, or avocado slices and topping with a light dressing.

Remember, the more color your vegetables have, the more nutrients they contain. Experts have known for decades about the positive effect vegetables have on our health. I will never forget a seminar I took part in at the University of Texas MD Anderson Cancer Center in Houston, where one of the scientific presenters stated a simple fact: Almost 30 percent of cancers can be avoided by including fruits and vegetables in your diet. These words have remained with me, because they make clear the impact these simple foods can have on one's life.

## Ensalada de Aguacate y Toronja

# AVOCADO AND GRAPEFRUIT SALAD

**◆· Serves 8 ·◆**

*I love this salad, because it's colorful and it combines vitamin C–rich Ruby Red grapefruit with heart-healthy avocados. The dressing pulls it all together and makes it even tastier. This salad goes well with many Mexican dishes, such as Pollo Fiesta con Hongos, Chiles y Cilantro (page 168).*

**CILANTRO-LIME DRESSING**

2 tablespoons fresh lime juice

2 tablespoons extra virgin olive oil

2 tablespoons finely chopped cilantro

1 garlic clove, minced

⅛ teaspoon salt

Black pepper, to taste

**SALAD**

4 Ruby Red grapefruit, peeled and sectioned

4 avocados, peeled, pitted, and sliced

¼ cup (10 g) chopped cilantro

**1.** To make the dressing, place all the ingredients in a blender or food processor and blend until smooth.

**2.** To assemble the salad, arrange alternating slices of the grapefruit and avocados on a plate. Drizzle with the dressing and garnish with the cilantro.

———

Per serving:

CALORIES 231; FAT 19 g (sat 3 g); PROTEIN 3 g; CARB 18 g; FIBER 4 g;
SUGARS 11 g; SODIUM 47 mg

# Ensalada de Repollo con Jícama y Zanahoria
## CABBAGE SALAD WITH JICAMA AND CARROTS
### ⟵· Serves 6 ·⟶

*The cabbage, tomatoes, and carrots in this recipe are loaded with vitamins, such as vitamins A and C. This fiber-rich salad will also leave you satisfied! Add grilled chicken or your protein of choice for a complete meal.*

**LIME VINAIGRETTE**

¼ cup (60 ml) fresh lime juice

¼ cup (60 ml) white wine vinegar

2 tablespoons olive oil

⅛ teaspoon dry mustard

**SALAD**

½ head green cabbage, shredded

2 medium tomatoes, seeded and diced

2 celery ribs, chopped

1 small sweet onion, thinly sliced

1 medium carrot, peeled and shredded

½ medium jicama, peeled and julienned

¼ cup (10 g) chopped cilantro

¼ cup (40 g) raisins

4 avocados, peeled, pitted, and sliced

**1.** To make the dressing, mix all the ingredients together in a small bowl. Set aside.

**2.** To assemble the salad, combine the cabbage, tomatoes, celery, onion, carrot, jicama, cilantro, and raisins in a large bowl. Add the dressing and toss gently. Top with the avocado slices and serve immediately.

———

Per serving:
CALORIES 332; FAT 25 g (sat 4 g); PROTEIN 5 g; CARB 28 g; FIBER 12 g;
SUGARS 12 g; SODIUM 52 mg

### Ensalada de Zanahoria con Cilantro
# CARROT-CILANTRO SALAD
#### ➻· Serves 6 ·➻

*If you have to fix up something good in a hurry, try this simple recipe for something different. If you have time to chill this beforehand, though, it's worth it. Carrots are a fabulous source of vitamin A, which is good for your skin and eyes.*

5 carrots, peeled and cut into thin rounds

2 tablespoons finely chopped cilantro

¼ cup (60 ml) fat-free Catalina dressing

Combine the ingredients in a medium bowl. Refrigerate for 1 to 2 hours to allow the flavors to blend, then serve.

———

Per serving:
CALORIES 34; FAT 0 g (sat 0 g); PROTEIN 1 g; CARB 8 g; FIBER 2 g;
SUGARS 6 g; SODIUM 125 mg

## Ensalada de Repollo con Aderezo de Aguacate

# CABBAGE SALAD WITH AVOCADO DRESSING

**◆· Serves 8 ·◆**

*This salad is so simple and keeps well in the refrigerator for two to three days. Cabbage is rich in vitamins A, C, E, and K, as well as fiber. This recipe combines this nutritious vegetable with heart-healthy avocado, which forms a creamy, delicious dressing!*

One 10-ounce (283 g) package shredded cabbage (about 4 cups)

½ large avocado

2 tablespoons fresh lime juice

1 tablespoon olive oil

½ teaspoon salt

¼ teaspoon black pepper

½ cup (100 g) diced tomatoes

**1.** Place the cabbage in a large bowl.

**2.** In a separate bowl, mash the avocado, then mix in the lime juice, oil, salt, and pepper until well blended.

**3.** Add to the cabbage and mix well. Just before serving, add the tomatoes and toss to combine.

———

Per serving:
CALORIES 48; FAT 4 g (sat 1 g); PROTEIN 1 g; CARB 4 g; FIBER 2 g;
SUGARS 2 g; SODIUM 154 mg

## Ensalada Romaine con Aderezo de Lima

# ROMAINE SALAD WITH SPICY LIME DRESSING

**→· Serves 6 ·→**

*I love preparing this salad to accompany heavier Mexican dishes. It's colorful and contains lots of nutrients, such as vitamins A and C and potassium. It also has a good amount of fiber and monounsaturated fat. Don't have time to make the salad dressing? There are many options for lime dressings available at the grocery store. Chop your romaine into bite-sized pieces—your guests will love it. This salad goes well with Pollo Rancho King (page 172).*

**SPICY LIME DRESSING**

⅓ cup (80 ml) extra virgin olive oil

⅓ cup (80 ml) fresh lime juice

2 dashes hot sauce, such as Tabasco

½ teaspoon salt

⅛ teaspoon black pepper

**SALAD**

1 large head romaine lettuce, chopped into bite-sized pieces

1 large tomato, seeded and diced

½ English cucumber, sliced

½ red onion, diced

1 cup fresh roasted corn kernels (165 g) or frozen kernels (135 g), thawed

⅔ cup (25 g) chopped cilantro

1 avocado, peeled, pitted, and diced

**1.** To make the dressing, combine all the ingredients in a jar with a tight-fitting lid. Shake vigorously to blend well.

**2.** To assemble the salad, combine all the ingredients except the avocado in a large bowl. Just before serving, add the avocado. Add the dressing and toss well.

———

Per serving:
CALORIES 209; FAT 19 g (sat 3 g); PROTEIN 3 g; CARB 12 g; FIBER 4 g; SUGARS 3 g; SODIUM 209 mg

## Ensalada de Pepino y Tomate
# CUCUMBER TOMATO SALAD
**▸· Serves 4 ·◂**

*If you need an easy salad to go with your Mexican meal, this fits the bill. It takes just a few minutes to prepare and looks so nice on a platter. Serve it alongside Enchiladas de Chile Colorado (page 199) or Pollo Adobado (page 171).*

Lettuce leaves

2 large English cucumbers, peeled in stripes and sliced into rounds

4 Roma tomatoes, sliced into thin rounds

2 tablespoons fresh lime juice

Black pepper, to taste

Line a large platter with enough lettuce leaves to cover the bottom. Arrange the cucumbers and tomatoes on top, then drizzle the lime juice over the vegetables and dust lightly with black pepper.

———

Per serving:
CALORIES 34; FAT 0 g (sat 0 g); PROTEIN 2 g; CARB 7 g; FIBER 2 g;
SUGARS 2 g; SODIUM 9 mg

Ensalada de Coditos con Cilantro
# CILANTRO PASTA SALAD
### ←·· Serves 8 ··→

*This salad tastes wonderful when prepared with whole wheat pasta, which is always a better choice, because it contains more fiber and nutrients. Fiber makes you feel full longer, and it can help to lower cholesterol.*

8 ounces (227 g) whole wheat elbow macaroni or other small pasta

⅔ cup (165 g) low-fat plain yogurt

¼ cup (10 g) chopped cilantro

1 serrano chile, chopped, seeded, and stemmed

1 garlic clove

½ teaspoon salt

¼ cup (30 g) chopped red onion

**1.** Prepare the pasta per package directions. Drain and allow to cool slightly.

**2.** Place the yogurt, cilantro, chile, garlic, and salt in a blender or food processor. Process for 45 to 60 seconds, until all the ingredients have blended well.

**3.** Transfer the cooled macaroni and dressing to a large bowl and toss with the onion. Refrigerate for 3 to 4 hours to allow the flavors to blend.

———

Per serving:
CALORIES 111; FAT 1 g (sat 0 g); PROTEIN 5 g; CARB 23 g; FIBER 2 g;
SUGARS 3 g; SODIUM 161 mg

## Ensalada de Garbanzo Rio Grande
# RIO GRANDE CHICKPEA SALAD

**←· Serves 4 ·→**

*This salad is colorful and so easy to prepare. It contains chickpeas, which are high in soluble fiber that can help lower blood cholesterol and help you feel full longer. They're also a good source of protein.*

¼ cup (60 ml) white wine vinegar

1 tablespoon extra virgin olive oil

1 garlic clove, finely minced

2 tablespoons chopped cilantro

One 15-ounce (425 g) can chickpeas, drained and rinsed

½ cup (80 g) finely chopped red onion

¼ cup (50 g) pimientos, drained

**1.** Combine the vinegar, oil, garlic, and cilantro in a medium bowl.

**2.** Add the chickpeas, onion, and pimientos and mix well. Cover and refrigerate, stirring occasionally, for at least 3 hours.

———

Per serving:
CALORIES 135; FAT 5 g (sat 0 g); PROTEIN 5 g; CARB 25 g; FIBER 5 g;
SUGARS 4 g; SODIUM 138 mg

## Ensalada de Frijol Pinto
# PINTO BEAN SALAD
### ← · Serves 8 · →

*This is a great summer salad! Canned beans are usually a better choice for this recipe, because they tend to be firmer than freshly cooked ones. Rinse them in a colander to remove some of the sodium and starchy liquid.*

¼ cup (10 g) finely chopped cilantro

¼ cup (60 ml) fresh lime juice

2 tablespoons olive oil

4 cups (680 g) drained, rinsed canned pinto beans (about three 15-ounce/425 g cans)

½ cup (60 g) chopped red onion

Lettuce leaves

2 medium tomatoes, quartered

**1.** Combine the cilantro, lime juice, and oil in a small container with a lid. Cover and shake to blend well.

**2.** Combine the beans and onion in a large bowl and toss with the dressing. Chill for at least 3 hours or overnight to allow the flavors to blend.

**3.** Divide among bowls lined with enough lettuce leaves to cover the bottom and garnish with the tomato wedges.

———

Per serving:
CALORIES 143; FAT 4 g (sat 1 g); PROTEIN 7 g; CARB 21 g; FIBER 5 g;
SUGARS  g; SODIUM 183 mg

## Ensalada de Jícama
# JICAMA SALAD
### ← · Serves 4 · →

*Jicamas have a cool, crisp taste. Peel the jicama much as you would a potato, removing the outer skin. Combining the jicama with apples and tossing in a citrus dressing makes a wonderful salad that is a great accompaniment for Pollo Adobado (page 171). It can also be served as a light appetizer.*

Lettuce leaves

⅓ cup (80 ml) fresh lime juice

1 teaspoon sugar

⅛ teaspoon salt

2 large apples, cored and sliced into thin wedges

½ small jicama, peeled and sliced into thin wedges

1 teaspoon chili powder (optional)

**1.** Line a large platter with enough lettuce leaves to cover the bottom.

**2.** Mix the lime juice, sugar, and salt in a large bowl. Add the apples and jicama and toss to combine.

**3.** Arrange the mixture, alternating apples and jicama, on the lettuce leaves. Dust lightly with chili powder, if desired.

———

Per serving:
CALORIES 92; FAT 0 g (sat 0 g); PROTEIN 1 g; CARB 23 g; FIBER 5 g;
SUGARS 16 g; SODIUM 73 mg

### Ensalada Mexicana de Fiesta
# MEXICAN FIESTA SALAD
**➤· Serves 8 ·➤**

*This salad has lots of soluble fiber, vitamins A and C, and heart-healthy fats from the avocado. Soluble fiber helps to lower cholesterol by binding it in the GI tract. Add grilled chicken or shrimp for a more substantial meal, or try this salad with Albóndigas de Salmón (page 152).*

1 head romaine lettuce, torn into bite-sized pieces

2 medium tomatoes, seeded and chopped

1 carrot, peeled and shredded

1 cup (175 g) drained, rinsed canned kidney beans

½ cup (75 g) finely chopped green bell pepper

½ small red onion, sliced into rings

1 avocado, peeled, pitted, and chopped

½ cup (60 ml) fat-free Catalina dressing

Gently toss together the lettuce, tomatoes, carrot, beans, pepper, and onion. Just before serving, top with the avocado and dressing.

————

Per serving:
CALORIES 100; FAT 4 g (sat 1 g); PROTEIN 3 g; CARB 14 g; FIBER 4 g;
SUGARS 6 g; SODIUM 216 mg

# Ensalada de Elote
# MEXICAN STREET CORN SALAD
**►· Serves 10 ·◄**

*In Mexico, it's common to see street vendors selling elotes, roasted corn on the cob seasoned with lime, chili powder, and mayonnaise. This delicious salad has many of the same flavors. To add a little crunch, top it with crushed baked tortilla chips (Tortillas Doradas, page 107). Add diced avocado for even more flavor!*

½ cup (110 g) light mayonnaise

½ cup (120 g) low-fat plain Greek yogurt

¼ cup (60 ml) fresh lime juice

2 teaspoons chili powder

1½ teaspoons salt

1 tablespoon olive oil

5 cups (675 g) frozen corn kernels, thawed

½ cup (50 g) chopped scallions

¼ cup (35 g) chopped red bell pepper

¼ cup (10 g) chopped cilantro

Cotija (optional)

Baked tortilla chips, crushed (Tortillas Doradas, page 107; optional)

**1.** Combine the mayonnaise, yogurt, lime juice, chili powder, and salt in a medium bowl. Set aside.

**2.** Heat the oil in a large skillet over medium-high heat. Add the corn and cook until it starts to brown, 10 to 12 minutes, stirring occasionally.

**3.** Transfer the corn to a large bowl. Add the scallions, pepper, cilantro, and dressing, mix well, and refrigerate for 2 hours to allow the flavors to blend.

**3.** Just before serving, top with cotija or crushed baked tortilla chips, if desired.

Per serving:
CALORIES 120; FAT 5 g (sat 1 g); PROTEIN 3 g; CARB 17 g; FIBER 2 g;
SUGARS 2 g; SODIUM 446 mg

## Ensalada de Espinaca Mexicana
# MEXICAN SPINACH SALAD
### ←· Serves 6 ·→

*Spinach is an excellent source of vitamin A. In this salad, it's combined with jicama for added crunch. You can also add grated carrots and avocado for an even more nutritious option.*

**YOGURT-CILANTRO DRESSING**

⅔ cup (165 g) low-fat plain yogurt

⅓ cup (15 g) chopped cilantro

1 serrano chile, stemmed, seeded, and chopped

1 garlic clove, chopped

¼ teaspoon salt

**SALAD**

10 ounces (285 g) fresh baby spinach

½ small jicama, peeled and julienned

12 cherry tomatoes, halved

2 ounces (55 g) reduced-fat Monterey Jack, grated (½ cup)

4 scallions, thinly sliced

**1.** To make the dressing, place all the ingredients in a blender or food processor and blend for 45 to 60 seconds, until combined.

**2.** To assemble the salad, gently toss together the spinach, jicama, tomatoes, cheese, and scallions in a large bowl. Serve with the dressing on the side.

————

Per serving:
CALORIES 80; FAT 2 g (sat 2 g); PROTEIN 5 g; CARB 11 g; FIBER 4 g;
SUGARS 4 g; SODIUM 274 mg

## Ensalada de Nopalitos
# NOPALITOS SALAD
### ←· Serves 4 ·→

*Nopales are young cactus pads. They have a mild flavor, and they can be eaten cooked in savory or sweet dishes. They are often mixed with scrambled eggs (nopalitos con huevos). They can even be made into jam. Nopales are rich in fiber and good sources of antioxidants. When chopped they are known as nopalitos.*

2 cups nopalitos, cleaned and cut into 1-inch (2.5 cm) pieces

1 medium tomato, seeded and roughly chopped

½ cup (60 g) roughly chopped onion

¼ cup (10 g) chopped cilantro

1 tablespoon fresh lime juice

½ teaspoon salt

½ teaspoon black pepper

Combine all the ingredients in a large bowl and toss gently. Refrigerate for 3 to 4 hours before serving.

———

Per serving:
CALORIES 22; FAT 0 g (sat 0 g); PROTEIN 1 g; CARB 5 g; FIBER 2 g;
SUGARS 2 g; SODIUM 304 mg

## Ensalada de Pollo
# CHICKEN TACO SALAD
### ➤· Serves 4 ·➤

*Most health experts recommend incorporating more vegetables and legumes into our diets. This delicious salad features beans and tomatoes, which are great sources of fiber and vitamins. This is a great recipe to use up leftover chicken. Warming it in the Pico de Gallo (page 34) adds more flavor.*

1 tablespoon olive oil

1 pound (455 g) chicken breast meat, sliced

1 cup (170 g) Pico de Gallo (page 34) or salsa of choice

4 cups (140 g) shredded romaine lettuce

2 medium tomatoes, seeded and chopped

½ medium red onion, chopped

24 baked tortilla chips (from 4 corn tortillas: Tortillas de Maíz, page 105) or store-bought baked chips

One 15-ounce (425 g) can kidney or black beans, drained and rinsed

3 ounces (85 g) reduced-fat cheddar, grated (¾ cup)

**1.** Heat the oil in a medium skillet over low heat, then add the chicken. Cook over low heat, then add the pico de gallo. Cover and simmer until the chicken is cooked through, 8 to 10 minutes. If the chicken gets too dry, add a little water to the pan. Shred the chicken with a fork, then let cool in the refrigerator.

**2.** To serve, arrange the lettuce, tomatoes, and onion in a large bowl and place the shredded chicken on top. Top with the tortilla chips, beans, and cheese.

———

Per serving:
CALORIES 382; FAT 12 g (sat 4 g); PROTEIN 39 g; CARB 30 g; FIBER 7 g;
SUGARS 6 g; SODIUM 619 mg

## Ensalada de Atún en Aguacate
# MEXICAN TUNA SALAD IN AVOCADO

**⟶· Serves 2 ·⟵**

*Nutrition experts recommend that we eat at least two meals a week that include certain types of fish, such as salmon, tuna, and mackerel. Serving this salad in a superfood avocado makes it doubly nutritious.*

1 tablespoon light mayonnaise

1 teaspoon fresh lime juice

One 5-ounce (142 g) can water-packed white albacore tuna, drained

1 egg, hard-boiled and diced

½ celery rib, diced

½ Roma tomato, seeded and diced

2 teaspoons minced onion

1 serrano chile, diced (optional)

1 avocado, halved and pitted

Baked tortilla chips (Tortillas Doradas, page 107)

**1.** Mix together the mayonnaise and lime juice in a small bowl.

**2.** Mix the tuna, egg, celery, tomato, onion, and chile, if using, in a medium bowl. Add the mayonnaise mixture and stir to combine.

**3.** Spoon into the avocado halves and serve with the baked chips.

———

Per serving (without chile or chips):
CALORIES 288; FAT 21 g (sat 4 g); PROTEIN 20 g; CARB 9 g; FIBER 5 g; SUGARS 2 g; SODIUM 378 mg

## CARNES ~ MEAT

Tacos de Res con Salsa Tomatillo
### STEAK TACOS WITH TOMATILLO SAUCE
143

Carne Guisada
### SPICY BRAISED BEEF
144

Carne con Papas
### MEXICAN MEAT AND POTATO STEW
145

Posole de Puerco y Pollo
### PORK AND CHICKEN POSOLE
147

Tacos de Puerco Pernil en Olla de Cocción Lenta
### SLOW COOKER PORK PERNIL TACOS
149

## PESCADO ~ FISH

Huachinango Verde
### RED SNAPPER IN TOMATILLO SAUCE
150

Albóndigas de Salmón
### MEXICAN SALMON CAKES
152

Bacalao Mexicano
### MEXICAN COD STEAKS
153

Salmón Rostizado con Chipotle
### GRILLED CHIPOTLE SALMON
154

Tacos de Pescado con Ensalada de Repollo
### FISH TACOS WITH CILANTRO SLAW
157

Pez Espada con Salsa Casera
### SWORDFISH STEAKS WITH SALSA
159

# CARNES Y PESCADO

# MEAT & FISH

**M**eal preparation should be simple, with a focus on good nutrition. These recipes are, for the most part, easy to prepare. Until fairly recently, experts believed that that we needed to eat large portions of meat with every meal. But current recommendations indicate that meats should make up a small part of our diet. One 3- to 4-ounce (85 to 115 g) serving—that's about the size of the palm of your hand—at lunch and dinner is really all we need to meet our protein needs. Most of your meal should consist of grains and vegetables. The following recipes incorporate lean cuts of meat prepared with salsas, vegetables, and spices. There are also numerous recipes that feature fish as the main protein. There are many economical and delicious ways to prepare fish to make your diet healthier.

· · · · · · · · · · · · · · · · · · · · · · · · · · · · **HEALTHY EASY MEXICAN** · · · · · · · · · · · · · · · · · · · · · · · · · · · ·

140

## Tacos de Res con Salsa Tomatillo

# STEAK TACOS WITH TOMATILLO SAUCE

**⟶· Serves 4 ·⟵**

*This recipe tastes great with Arroz Blanco con Elote y Cebolla (page 214) and a salad. You can substitute chicken or pork loin for the beef . . . or just make the tacos with vegetables!*

1 tablespoon olive or canola oil

8 ounces (225 g) white mushrooms, thinly sliced

1 medium tomato, seeded and diced

½ green bell pepper, diced

1 pound (455 g) lean round steak, excess fat trimmed, thinly sliced

1 cup (240 ml) Roasted Tomatillo Sauce (Salsa de Tomatillo Tatemado, page 44), plus more for serving

½ teaspoon salt

½ teaspoon black pepper, or to taste

Corn tortillas (Tortillas de Maíz, page 105)

½ cup (120 g) low-fat plain Greek yogurt

**1.** Heat the oil in a large nonstick skillet over medium heat. Sauté the mushrooms, tomato, and bell pepper until tender, 5 to 7 minutes. Transfer to a plate and set aside.

**2.** In the same skillet, sauté the beef over medium-high heat until browned, 7 to 10 minutes. Add the cooked vegetables, then the tomatillo sauce, salt, and black pepper. Cover and simmer for 20 minutes, to allow the flavors to blend.

**3.** Warm the tortillas on a griddle or large skillet. Keep warm.

**4.** When ready to serve, divide the meat and vegetable mixture among the tortillas. Serve with a dollop of the yogurt and top with extra tomatillo sauce, if desired.

———

Per serving (with 2 tortillas):
CALORIES 346; FAT 11 g (sat 3 g); PROTEIN 34 g; CARB 31 g; FIBER 5 g;
SUGARS 4 g; SODIUM 844 mg

· · · · · · · · · · · · · · · · · · · · · · · · · · · **MEAT & FISH** · · · · · · · · · · · · · · · · · · · · · · · · · · ·

143

## Carne Guisada
# SPICY BRAISED BEEF
### ← · Serves 8 · →

*Serve this special dish with Frijoles de Olla (page 223), Arroz Mexicano (page 213), and fresh corn tortillas (Tortillas de Maíz, page 105). Preparing it with a cut of lean beef makes this recipe healthier than regular carne guisada, which is often made with fattier cuts of meat.*

3 large tomatoes, chopped

1 small onion, chopped

½ green bell pepper, seeded and chopped

3 garlic cloves, chopped

1 teaspoon salt

½ teaspoon chili powder

½ teaspoon ground cumin

⅛ teaspoon dried Mexican oregano

3 pounds (1.3 kg) lean round steak, excess fat trimmed, cut into 1-inch (2.5 cm) pieces

**1.** Place the tomatoes, onion, pepper, garlic, salt, chili powder, cumin, and oregano in a blender or food processor and blend until smooth. Set aside.

**2.** Place the steak in a Dutch oven or large pot over medium-high heat and cook until browned, 7 to 10 minutes, then drain the excess fat. Add the vegetable mixture and bring to a boil. Reduce the heat, cover, and simmer until the meat is tender, about 45 minutes.

———

Per serving:
CALORIES 247; FAT 7 g (sat 2 g); PROTEIN 39 g; CARB 5 g; FIBER 1 g;
SUGARS 3 g; SODIUM 388 mg

## Carne con Papas

# MEXICAN MEAT AND POTATO STEW

### ➼• Serves 4 •➼

*I love one-pot (or nearly one-pot) meals. Add a salad or some Guacamole con Comino Tostado (page 49) for a complete meal.*

1 tablespoon olive or other vegetable oil

1 pound (455 g) lean round steak, excess fat trimmed, cut into 2-inch (5 cm) pieces

3 medium white potatoes, peeled if desired, cut into 1-inch (2.5 cm) cubes

½ cup (120 ml) Mexican Spice Blend (Especias Mexicanas, page 24)

¼ cup (60 ml) no-salt-added tomato sauce

3 garlic cloves, minced

1 teaspoon salt

**1.** Heat the oil in a Dutch oven or large pot over medium heat. Brown the steak until all of the juices have evaporated and the meat no longer looks pink, 8 to 10 minutes. Add the potatoes, spice blend, tomato sauce, garlic, salt, and 2½ cups (720 ml) water.

**2.** Bring to a boil, then reduce the heat and simmer until the potatoes are tender, about 30 minutes.

―――――

Per serving:
CALORIES 237; FAT 8 g (sat 2 g); PROTEIN 29 g; CARB 10 g; FIBER 5 g;
SUGARS  g; SODIUM 656 mg

### Posole de Puerco y Pollo
# PORK AND CHICKEN POSOLE
#### ← · Serves 8 · →

*Traditional Mexican posole is a brothy soup that is rich in spices. Typically, posole is made with pork shoulder, a fatty cut of pork. This recipe is lower in fat, prepared with chicken breast and lean pork for flavor. Posole, often served during the holidays, is accompanied by some rather unexpected toppings, such as sliced radishes. To serve, set out small bowls with shredded cabbage, sliced radishes, chopped onions, avocados, and cilantro. After you've garnished your posole, add just a squeeze of lime juice for a delicious pop of flavor.*

1 tablespoon olive oil

1 medium onion, finely chopped

2 garlic cloves, minced

1¼ pounds (565 g) chicken breast meat, cooked and shredded

4 ounces (115 g) pork tenderloin, cooked and shredded

Two 29-ounce (822 g) cans white hominy, drained and rinsed (about 7 cups)

½ cup (120 ml) Mexican Spice Blend (Especias Mexicanas, page 24), or to taste

2 tablespoons chili powder

1½ teaspoons salt

¼ teaspoon dried Mexican oregano

2 tablespoons masa harina

Thinly sliced radishes

Shredded cabbage

Chopped cilantro

Lime wedges

**1.** Heat the oil in a Dutch oven or large pot over medium heat. Add the onion and sauté until translucent, 5 to 6 minutes. Add the garlic and sauté for 1 more minute.

**2.** Add the chicken and pork and warm slightly, about 5 minutes. Add the hominy, spice blend, chili powder, salt, oregano, and 7½ cups (1.8 L) water and stir to combine.

**3.** Bring to a boil, then reduce the heat, cover, and simmer for 30 minutes, until heated through and the flavors have blended. Taste and adjust seasonings.

**4.** Mix the masa harina and ½ cup (120 ml) water in a small bowl. Add to the pot and stir to prevent lumps from forming. Allow to simmer until the broth thickens slightly, about 20 minutes.

**5.** Serve with shredded cabbage, radishes, cilantro, and lime wedges.

———

Per serving (without garnish):
CALORIES 236; FAT 5 g (sat 1 g); PROTEIN 22 g; CARB 25 g; FIBER 5 g;
SUGARS 2 g; SODIUM 812 mg

# Tacos de Puerco Pernil en Olla de Cocción Lenta
# SLOW COOKER PORK PERNIL TACOS

**↞· Serves 12 ·↠**

*Pernil is a traditional slow-cooked pork shoulder roast in Latin Caribbean countries. In this Cuban-inspired version, a simple marinade of garlic, spices, and a blend of citrus juices infuse the pork before cooking. Because this recipe calls for a much leaner cut of pork, check it after four hours in the slow cooker—you don't want to overcook it. This recipe makes the most delectable tacos and is great served with Arroz con Elote y Cebolla (page 214).*

3 pounds (1.3 kg) pork tenderloin

5 or 6 garlic cloves, crushed

1 cup (240 ml) fresh orange juice (from about 3 oranges)

¼ cup (60 ml) fresh lime juice

1½ teaspoons ground cumin

1½ teaspoons salt

½ teaspoon dried Mexican oregano

¼ teaspoon black pepper

24 corn tortillas (Tortillas de Maíz, page 105)

Shredded lettuce

Chopped tomatoes

1 cup (120 g) crumbled queso blanco

**1.** Use a sharp knife to cut four slits into the pork and place four of the garlic cloves into the holes. Place the pork in a large zipper bag.

**2.** Combine the remaining garlic, orange juice, lime juice, cumin, salt, oregano, and pepper in a small bowl. Pour over the pork and seal the bag. Allow to marinate in the refrigerator for at least 12 hours, turning once.

**3.** Remove the pork from the refrigerator and allow to stand for about 30 minutes. Transfer the pork along with the marinade to a slow cooker and cook on low for 4 to 6 hours, until the pork reaches an internal temperature of 145°F (60°C). Check the temperature after about 3 hours.

**4.** Remove the pork, shred using two forks, and return to the slow cooker with the cooking liquid. Warm for about 15 minutes.

**5.** Serve on warm corn tortillas with lettuce, tomatoes, and the queso blanco.

---

Per serving (with 2 tortillas, no tomato or lettuce):
CALORIES 280; FAT 8 g (sat 1 g); PROTEIN 29 g; CARB 24 g; FIBER 3 g;
SUGARS 2 g; SODIUM 670 mg

## Huachinango Verde
# RED SNAPPER IN TOMATILLO SAUCE
### ·• Serves 8 •·

*Tomatillo sauce gives this fish a nice tangy flavor. You can substitute another type of fish, if you prefer.*

2 pounds (910 g) red snapper fillets

½ teaspoon salt

Black pepper

2 limes, thinly sliced

2 teaspoons olive oil

1 cup (240 ml) Roasted Tomatillo Sauce (Salsa de Tomatillo Tatemado, page 44), warmed

**1.** Line a baking sheet with foil. Place the fish on the baking sheet and sprinkle with the salt and pepper. Place the lime slices on the fillets. Cover with foil and refrigerate for 4 to 5 hours.

**3.** Preheat the oven to 400°F (200°C).

**4.** Brush the fillets with the oil. Bake for 30 minutes, or until the flesh turns opaque and flakes easily. Serve immediately with the tomatillo sauce.

———

Per serving:
CALORIES 135; FAT 3 g (sat 0 g); PROTEIN 24 g; CARB 2 g; FIBER 1 g;
SUGARS 0 g; SODIUM 328 mg

## Albóndigas de Salmón
# MEXICAN SALMON CAKES
### ⬖· Serves 2 ·⬖

*Albóndigas are a cost-effective way to get more fish into your diet. This version incorporates salmon, a fatty fish rich in heart-healthy fats, which can help prevent heart disease and strokes. They are also a good source of calcium. You can serve them with Crema de Aguacate (page 47), Crema Chipotle (page 46), or your favorite salsa. Keep a few cans of salmon in your pantry for a quick meal! These can also be prepared with canned tuna.*

½ cup (70 g) plain bread crumbs

Grated zest of 1 lemon

½ teaspoon salt

½ teaspoon black pepper

One 7.5-ounce (213 g) can pink salmon, drained, broken into bite-sized pieces

1 egg

¼ cup (40 g) minced onion

¼ cup (35 g) minced red bell pepper

1 tablespoon olive oil

**1.** Mix the bread crumbs, lemon zest, salt, and black pepper in a medium bowl. Add the salmon, egg, onion, and bell pepper and stir to combine. Divide the mixture into four patties.

**2.** Heat the oil in a large nonstick skillet over medium-high heat. Cook the patties for 4 to 5 minutes on each side, until they are golden brown.

————

Per serving:
CALORIES 355; FAT 15 g (sat 2 g); PROTEIN 24 g; CARB 29 g; FIBER 2 g;
SUGARS 3 g; SODIUM 1,277 mg

# Bacalao Mexicano
# MEXICAN COD STEAKS
## ← · Serves 4 · →

*Bell peppers are rich sources of vitamin C, and along with onions and garlic, they give this simple fish recipe plenty of flavor. Serve with Ensalada de Repollo con Aderezo de Aguacate (page 120) for a perfect meal.*

1 tablespoon olive oil

1 green bell pepper, thinly sliced

1 red bell pepper, thinly sliced

1 large onion, thinly sliced

2 tablespoons Mexican Spice Blend (Especias Mexicanas, page 24)

2 garlic cloves, crushed

½ teaspoon salt

4 cod fillets, about 4 ounces (115 g) each

**1.** Heat the oil in a large nonstick skillet over medium heat. Add the peppers and onion, followed by the spice blend, garlic, and salt, and sauté, stirring frequently, until the onion is translucent, 5 to 7 minutes. Remove from the pan and set aside. Do not wipe out the skillet.

**2.** Place the cod in the skillet, then arrange the vegetables on top. Cover and cook until the fish is opaque and flaky, 10 to 15 minutes.

———

Per serving:
CALORIES 137; FAT 5 g (sat 0 g); PROTEIN 21 g; CARB 4 g; FIBER 1 g;
SUGARS 1 g; SODIUM 372 mg

## Salmón Rostizado con Chipotle
# GRILLED CHIPOTLE SALMON

**━•· Serves 2 ·━**

*Salmon is a rich source of omega-3 fatty acids, which are believed to reduce inflammation in the body and decrease triglycerides. This salmon is also great in tacos, drizzled with Crema de Aguacate (page 47) and topped with slaw (see Cilantro Slaw, page 157).*

Two 5-ounce (140 g) skin-on salmon steaks, about 1 inch (2.5 cm) thick

¼ cup (60 ml) fresh lime juice

Nonstick cooking spray

½ cup (120 ml) no-salt-added tomato sauce

½ to 1 chipotle chile in adobo, or to taste

½ teaspoon salt

⅛ teaspoon black pepper

**1.** Place the salmon, skin side down, in a covered container with the lime juice. Place in the refrigerator to marinate for 1½ hours. Remove from the refrigerator and allow to come to room temperature before baking.

**2.** Preheat the oven to 350°F (180°C). Line a baking sheet with foil and spray with cooking spray.

**3.** Combine the tomato sauce and chipotle chile in adobo in a blender or food processor and blend until smooth.

**4.** Place the salmon, skin side down, on the baking sheet and season with the salt and pepper. Bake for about 20 minutes, until the thickest part of the salmon reaches 145°F (60°C). Serve with the chipotle sauce.

———

Per serving:
CALORIES 296; FAT 16 g (sat 3 g); PROTEIN 29 g; CARB 7 g; FIBER 2 g;
SUGARS 4 g; SODIUM 694 mg

## Tacos de Pescado con Ensalada de Repollo
# FISH TACOS WITH CILANTRO SLAW
### ← · Serves 8 · →

*These fish tacos are lightly sautéed in a pan with olive oil instead of breaded and fried. They are enhanced with this citrusy cumin slaw, which is cool and spicy at the same time; it goes perfectly with the fish and corn tortillas. Drizzle with Crema de Aguacate (page 47) or Crema Chipotle (page 46) for tacos with plenty of flavor!*

**CILANTRO SLAW**

¼ cup (60 ml) extra virgin olive oil

¼ cup (60 ml) apple cider vinegar

1 tablespoon grated orange zest

2 tablespoons fresh orange juice

1 teaspoon sugar

½ teaspoon ground cumin

½ teaspoon salt

Black pepper, to taste

2 cups (110 g) angel hair coleslaw mix

½ red bell pepper, finely chopped

1 cup (40 g) chopped cilantro

**FISH**

2 pounds (910 g) red snapper, tilapia, or other white fish fillets

2 teaspoons ancho chile powder

1 teaspoon salt

Black pepper

2 tablespoons olive oil

To serve

16 corn tortillas (Tortillas de Maíz, page 105)

Chopped cilantro

Lime wedges

**1.** To make the slaw, combine the oil, vinegar, orange zest and juice, sugar, cumin, salt, and black pepper in a jar with a lid. Shake to mix and set aside.

**2.** Combine the coleslaw mix, bell pepper, and cilantro in a medium bowl. Add the vinegar dressing and mix well. Refrigerate until ready to serve.

**3.** To make the fish, heat an electric griddle to 350°F (180°C) or heat a large skillet over medium-high heat.

**4.** Season the fish fillets with the chile powder, salt, and black pepper on both sides.

**5.** Heat the oil on the griddle and panfry the fish to form a nice crust, 3 to 4 minutes on each side, until the fish is opaque and flakes easily. Set aside.

**6.** Heat the tortillas on the griddle for 2 to 3 minutes on each side. Transfer to a tortilla warmer or a clean kitchen towel to keep warm.

**7.** Just before serving, flake the fish and place on the tortillas. Top with the slaw and more cilantro. Serve with lime wedges.

––––––––

Per serving:
CALORIES 313; FAT 13 g (sat 0 g); PROTEIN 26 g; CARB 24 g; FIBER 3 g;
SUGARS 2 g; SODIUM 489 mg

### Pez Espada con Salsa Casera

# SWORDFISH STEAKS WITH SALSA

**⇥· Serves 4 ·⇥**

*Swordfish is almost always sold as steaks. With jalapeño, tomatoes, and cilantro, this recipe adds a Mexican touch to this mild fish. Serve with Arroz con Comino (page 215) and a green salad.*

2 tablespoons olive oil

½ cup (60 g) chopped onion

2 garlic cloves, crushed

4 swordfish steaks, approximately 4 ounces (115 g) each

1 jalapeño, stemmed, seeded, and finely chopped

5 medium tomatoes, seeded and finely chopped

½ cup (20 g) chopped cilantro

1 tablespoon fresh lime juice

**1.** Heat 1 tablespoon of the oil in a large skillet over medium-high heat. Sauté the onion until translucent, about 5 minutes, then add the garlic and sauté for 1 more minute. Remove from the skillet and set aside.

**2.** Heat the remaining 1 tablespoon oil in the skillet, then add the swordfish and cook for 2 to 3 minutes on each side. The swordfish flesh should become opaque and flake easily. Remove from the skillet and keep warm.

**3.** Sauté the jalapeño in the skillet until tender, 2 to 3 minutes. Add the tomatoes, cilantro, and lime juice and continue to sauté, stirring frequently, until the tomatoes have softened, about 5 minutes. Add the garlic and onion and stir to combine. Spoon over the fish and serve.

———

Per serving:
CALORIES 241; FAT 12 g (sat 1 g); PROTEIN 24 g; CARB 10 g; FIBER 2 g;
SUGARS 5 g; SODIUM 119 mg

# POULTRY

Poultry is a great lean protein—and so versatile. When cooking chicken and turkey with a Mexican twist, the addition of fresh salsas, tangy tomatillos, cumin, and garlic takes these everyday proteins to new heights.

Want a quick lunch? Keep canned chicken breast in your pantry for a speedy salad. Or try some of the recipes from this chapter! One of my favorite casseroles for entertaining is the easy but delicious Pollo Rancho King (page 172), named after the famous ranch in deep South Texas. It can be made in advance and warmed just before mealtime.

It's important to remember that chicken and turkey skin actually contain a considerable amount of fat. Eating the skin can almost triple the calories. While cooking, you can keep the skin on to retain moisture, but pass on eating it for a lower-calorie option.

## Pollo Guisado
# SPICY BRAISED CHICKEN
#### ◄·• Serves 6 •·►

*This recipe is an adaptation of one of my mother's recipes—my children have all tested it and gave it rave reviews. You can add diced potatoes to this stew before simmering for a filling one-pot meal.*

1 tablespoon olive oil

1½ pounds (680 g) chicken breast meat, cut into 1-inch (2.5 cm) cubes

2 garlic cloves, crushed

¼ cup (60 ml) Mexican Spice Blend (Especias Mexicanas, page 24)

2 tablespoons no-salt-added tomato sauce

¾ teaspoon salt

2 tablespoons all-purpose flour

1 bay leaf

**1.** Heat the oil in a Dutch oven or large pot over medium heat. Add the chicken and cook until slightly browned and cooked through, 10 to 15 minutes.

**2.** Add the garlic and sauté for 1 minute. Add the spice blend, tomato sauce, and salt and stir to combine. Bring to a slight boil, then reduce the heat to low. Cover and simmer for about 5 minutes, until the tomato sauce has darkened in color.

**3.** Whisk the flour into 2 cups (480 ml) water to form a slurry. Add the slurry to the pot along with the bay leaf, stirring frequently to allow the sauce to thicken.

**4.** Bring to a boil, then reduce the heat to low and simmer for 15 minutes, until the flavors have blended and the chicken is tender.

———

Per serving:
CALORIES 160; FAT 4 g (sat 0 g); PROTEIN 27 g; CARB 3 g; FIBER 0 g; SUGARS 0 g; SODIUM 366 mg

# CHILAQUILES

**◄• Serves 4 •►**

*This recipe is so easy to make, and it's a great way to use leftover chicken and tortillas. Many of the ingredients are pantry staples. The sharp cheddar imparts flavor but not too much saturated fat. This casserole is best eaten for breakfast, brunch, or lunch. Serve it with avocado and a green salad or prepare it without the chicken for a great vegetarian meal.*

12 corn tortillas (Tortillas de Maiz, page 105)

2 tablespoons olive oil

1 medium yellow onion, diced

2 cloves garlic, minced

One 28-ounce (794 g) can no-salt-added petite diced tomatoes

One 14-ounce (397 g) can no-salt-added tomatoes and green chiles

¼ cup (10 g) chopped cilantro

2 teaspoons red chile powder

1 teaspoon ground cumin

¾ teaspoon salt

½ teaspoon black pepper

Nonstick cooking spray

2 cups (270 g) diced cooked chicken breast

6 ounces (170 g) reduced-fat sharp cheddar, grated (1½ cups)

**1.** Preheat the oven to 350°F (180°C). Line a baking sheet with foil.

**2.** Use 1 tablespoon of the oil to brush both sides of each tortilla. Cut each tortilla into six wedges and place on the baking sheet. Bake for 5 to 8 minutes, or just until crisp.

**3.** Heat the remaining 1 tablespoon oil in a large skillet over medium heat. Add the onion and sauté until translucent, 5 to 6 minutes. Add the garlic and sauté for 1 more minute.

**4.** Add the large can of tomatoes and their juices, breaking up large pieces using a potato masher or wooden spoon. Add the can of tomatoes and green chiles, the cilantro, red chile powder, cumin, salt, and pepper. Stir and bring to a boil. Simmer for about 8 minutes to allow the flavors to blend well.

**5.** Spray a 9 x 13-inch (23 x 33 cm) baking dish with cooking spray. Place half of the tortilla chips in a layer on the bottom, followed by half of the chicken, half of the sauce, and half of the cheese. Repeat with another layer of the chips, chicken, and sauce.

**6.** Bake for 10 minutes, add the remaining cheese and return to oven until heated through. Serve warm.

————

Per serving:
CALORIES 437; FAT 18 g (sat 6 g); PROTEIN 35 g; CARB 33 g; FIBER 8 g;
SUGARS 10 g; SODIUM 1,134 mg

## Pollo Fiesta con Hongos, Chiles y Cilantro

# CHICKEN FIESTA WITH MUSHROOMS, CHILES, AND CILANTRO

**◄·· Serves 6 ··►**

*I love this casserole because you can use leftover chicken and brown rice. When combined with the fresh vegetables and salsa and topped with cheese, it's a great weeknight meal.*

Nonstick cooking spray

1 tablespoon olive oil

2 cups (140 g) sliced white mushrooms

½ cup (120 g) drained canned diced green chiles

½ cup (50 g) sliced scallions, plus more for serving

¼ cup (10 g) chopped cilantro

1½ cups (360 ml) Ranchero Sauce (Salsa Ranchera, page 33) or salsa of choice

1 pound (455 g) chicken breast meat, cooked and shredded

2 cups (400 g) cooked brown rice

1 cup (245 g) low-fat plain yogurt

Paprika

4 ounces (115 g) reduced-fat sharp cheddar, grated (1 cup)

**1.** Preheat the oven to 350°F (180°C). Spray a shallow 2-quart (2 L) baking dish with cooking spray.

**2.** Heat the oil in a nonstick skillet over medium heat. Add the mushrooms, chiles, scallions, and cilantro. Cook until the mushrooms have cooked through, 4 to 5 minutes, then stir in the salsa and cook until most of the liquid has evaporated, 7 to 10 minutes.

**3.** Mix together the chicken, rice, yogurt, and vegetables in a medium bowl, then transfer to the baking dish. Sprinkle lightly with paprika and the reserved scallions.

**4.** Bake for 30 minutes. Add the cheese and return to the oven. Warm until the cheese has melted, 5 to 10 minutes.

-------

Per serving:
CALORIES 287; FAT 9 g (sat 4 g); PROTEIN 27 g; CARB 23 g; FIBER 3 g;
SUGARS 5 g; SODIUM 429 mg

## Pollo en Salsa Naranja en Olla de Cocción Lenta
# SLOW COOKER CHICKEN IN ORANGE SAUCE

**←· Serves 4 ·→**

*One-pot meals just make life easier. In this recipe, mixing orange juice and jalapeños with spices results in a sweet yet savory dish. The potatoes and orange juice make this dish rich in vitamin C and fiber.*

6 ounces (175 ml) frozen orange juice concentrate (half a 12-ounce/355 ml can)

¼ cup (120 ml) Mexican Spice Blend (Especias Mexicanas, page 24)

2 garlic cloves

1 small jalapeño, stemmed, seeded, and diced

1 teaspoon salt

½ teaspoon chili powder

Four 6-ounce (170 g) boneless, skinless chicken breasts

½ cup (60 g) chopped onion

8 small red potatoes, scrubbed and quartered

**1.** Place the orange juice concentrate, spice blend, garlic, jalapeño, salt, and chili powder in a blender or food processor and blend until smooth.

**2.** Place the chicken in a slow cooker and pour in the orange juice mixture. Add the onion and potatoes.

**3.** Cook for 6 hours on high, until the internal temperature reaches 160°F (70°C). Serve warm.

———

Per serving:
CALORIES 298; FAT 2 g (sat 1 g); PROTEIN 42 g; CARB 24 g; FIBER 4 g; SUGARS 15 g; SODIUM 702 mg

## Pollo Adobado
# CHICKEN IN ADOBO SAUCE
#### ━· Serves 6 ·━

*Adobo is a marinade made with chile, vinegar, and spices. Marinating chicken in these rich flavors overnight is well worth the effort. This recipe pairs well with Calabacitas (page 70).*

1 cup (120 g) chopped onion

½ cup (60 ml) low-sodium chicken broth

3 tablespoons chili powder

2 garlic cloves, chopped

1 tablespoon red wine vinegar

½ teaspoon ground cumin

½ teaspoon dried Mexican oregano

½ teaspoon salt

2 pounds (905 g) boneless, skinless chicken breasts

12 corn tortillas (Tortillas de Maíz, page 105), warmed

½ cup (50 g) finely chopped scallions

**1.** Place the onion, chicken broth, chili powder, garlic, vinegar, cumin, oregano, and salt in a blender or food processor and blend until smooth.

**2.** Pour half of the mixture into a large baking dish. Arrange the chicken breasts in the dish and pour the remaining mixture over the chicken. Cover and refrigerate overnight. Remove from the refrigerator about 30 minutes before baking.

**3.** Preheat the oven to 350°F (180°C). Bake the chicken, covered, for 30 minutes. Uncover and bake for about 10 minutes, basting occasionally with the sauce, until the internal temperature is 165°F (75°C).

**4.** Shred the chicken with two forks, then return the chicken to the dish and bake for 15 minutes, to warm thoroughly.

**5.** Serve on warm corn tortillas and top with the scallions.

———

Per serving:
CALORIES 286; FAT 4 g (sat 1 g); PROTEIN 38 g; CARB 26 g; FIBER 5 g;
SUGARS 2 g; SODIUM 594 mg

## Pollo Rancho King
# KING RANCH CHICKEN
### ⤙· Serves 8 ·⤚

*This popular Texas favorite is named after the King Ranch, a legendary 800,000-acre ranch in South Texas. This version is much lower in fat and sodium than the original and makes a wonderful meal accompanied by Ensalada Romaine con Aderezo de Lima (page 122). This is a great meal for entertaining because it can easily be made ahead. It's definitely a crowd favorite!*

Nonstick cooking spray

2 tablespoons olive oil

1½ cups (105 g) sliced white mushrooms

1 cup (120 g) chopped onion

3 tablespoons all-purpose flour

2 cups (480 ml) reduced-sodium chicken broth

2 cups (480 ml) skim milk

1 teaspoon salt

½ teaspoon garlic powder

One 10-ounce (283 g) can no-salt-added diced tomatoes and green chiles (such as Ro-Tel), drained

One 4-ounce (113 g) can green chiles

¼ cup (10 g) chopped cilantro

4 cups (540 g) shredded cooked chicken breast

12 corn tortillas (Tortillas de Maíz, page 105), cut into eighths

11 ounces (310 g) reduced-fat cheddar, grated (2¾ cups)

**1.** Preheat the oven to 350°F (180°C). Spray a 9 x 13-inch (23 x 33 cm) baking dish with cooking spray.

**2.** Heat the oil in a large skillet over medium heat. Add the mushrooms and onion and sauté until the onion is translucent and the mushrooms have cooked through, about 5 minutes.

**3.** Add the flour and mix well. Cook for 4 minutes, stirring often. Add the broth, milk, salt, and garlic powder and blend well. Cook over medium heat until the mixture thickens, 7 to 10 minutes, stirring often. Add the tomatoes, green chiles, and cilantro. Mix well and remove from the heat.

**4.** Place half of the chicken in a layer on the bottom the baking dish. Add a layer of half the tortillas, followed by a layer of half the sauce and a layer of half the cheddar. Repeat with the remaining chicken, tortillas, and sauce. Set aside the remaining half of the cheddar.

**5.** Bake for 20 minutes. Remove from the oven and layer the remaining cheddar on top. Return to the oven and bake 5 to 10 minutes, until the casserole is bubbling and the cheese has melted.

———

Per serving:
CALORIES 375; FAT 15 g (sat 6 g); PROTEIN 34 g; CARB 26 g; FIBER 4 g;
SUGARS 5 g; SODIUM 1,011 mg

## Enchiladas Suizas
# TOMATILLO CHICKEN ENCHILADAS

**➤· Serves 6 ·➤**

*You can prepare these cheesy chicken enchiladas early in the day by rolling the enchiladas and refrigerating. The sauce can also be made ahead of time. Add the sauce to the enchiladas just before heating. You can omit the chicken breast if you want to make it meatless—just increase the amount of cheese. Serve with Frijoles de Olla (page 223).*

Nonstick cooking spray

12 ounces (340 g) reduced-fat Monterey Jack, grated (about 3 cups)

1¼ pounds (565 g) chicken breast meat, cooked and shredded

1 cup (140 g) finely chopped onion (cooked, if desired)

3 cups (720 ml) Simple Tomatillo Sauce (Salsa de Tomatillo Sencilla, page 42)

12 corn tortillas (store-bought is best)

Reduced-fat sour cream (optional)

**1.** Preheat the oven to 350°F (180°C). Spray a 9 x 13-inch (23 x 33 cm) baking dish with cooking spray.

**2.** Reserve about ½ cup (55 g) of the Monterey Jack. Combine the remaining cheese with the chicken and onion in a medium bowl.

**3.** Pour ½ cup (120 ml) of the tomatillo sauce into the bottom of the prepared dish.

**4.** Place the tortillas, six at a time, between clean damp kitchen towels and microwave for about 1 minute, until softened.

**5.** Lay a tortilla flat on a plate or cutting board. Place about 2 tablespoons of the chicken filling on the lower edge of the tortilla. Roll the tortilla, then place it seam side down in the baking dish. Repeat with the remaining tortillas, then pour the remaining sauce over the top, making sure the sauce gets between each one.

**6.** Bake for 10 minutes. Top with the reserved cheese and bake for 10 minutes, or until slightly bubbly.

**7.** Serve topped with a small dollop of sour cream, if desired.

———

Per serving (without sour cream):
CALORIES 484; FAT 22 g (sat 9 g); PROTEIN 40 g; CARB 36 g; FIBER 6 g;
SUGARS 2 g; SODIUM 627 mg

Enchiladas de Pollo en Salsa de Chile Ancho

# CHICKEN ENCHILADAS IN ANCHO CHILE SAUCE

### ← • Serves 6 • →

*If you truly want to taste the flavors of Mexico, try these enchiladas. They have a smoky, earthy flavor from the ancho chiles. Because each enchilada only contains a small amount of cheese, this recipe incorporates full-fat Monterey Jack. It is always best to grate your own cheese, because store-bought grated cheese contains additives and is more expensive. I hope you try these enchiladas—they're so good!*

1 tablespoon olive oil

½ medium yellow onion, minced

2½ cups (600 ml) Ancho Chile Sauce (Salsa de Chile Ancho, page 38)

12 corn tortillas (store-bought is best)

1½ pounds (680 g) chicken breast, cooked and shredded

4 ounces (115 g) Monterey Jack, grated (1 cup)

**1.** Preheat the oven to 350°F (180°C). Spray a 9 x 13-inch (23 x 33 cm) baking dish with cooking spray.

**2.** Heat the oil in a small skillet over medium heat. Cook the onions until translucent, about 5 minutes. Remove from the heat and set aside.

**3.** Pour ¼ cup (60 ml) of the chile sauce into the bottom of the prepared dish.

**4.** Place the tortillas, six at a time, between clean damp kitchen towels, and microwave for about 1 minute, until softened.

**5.** Lay a tortilla flat on a plate or cutting board. Place 1 teaspoon of the chicken, 1 tablespoon of the cheese, and 1 teaspoon of the onion on the lower edge of the tortilla. Roll the tortilla, then place it seam side down in the baking dish.

**6.** Repeat with the remaining tortillas, then pour the remaining sauce over the top, making sure the sauce gets between each one.

**7.** Bake for 10 minutes. Remove from the oven and top with the remaining ¼ cup of the cheese. Return to the oven and bake for 10 minutes, or until the cheese is melted and the sauce is bubbling slightly.

———

Per serving:
CALORIES 393; FAT 13 g (sat 5 g); PROTEIN 36 g; CARB 35 g; FIBER 7 g;
SUGARS 0 g; SODIUM 1,081 mg

· · · · · · · · · · · · · · · · · · · · · · · · · · **HEALTHY EASY MEXICAN** · · · · · · · · · · · · · · · · · · · · · · · · ·

176

## Calabaza con Pollo

# CHICKEN WITH MEXICAN SQUASH

**→·  Serves 6  ·→**

*Tatuma squash is tender and delicious cooked with chicken or lean pork. Tomatoes, green bell peppers, and corn make this meal rich in fiber and full of vitamin C. Serve with Frijoles de Olla (page 223) and fresh corn tortillas.*

1 tablespoon plus 1½ teaspoons olive oil

6 boneless, skinless chicken thighs, trimmed and cut into 1-inch (2.5 cm) pieces

1 large tomato, chopped

1 cup fresh (155 g) or frozen (135 g) corn kernels, thawed

1 small yellow onion, chopped

½ cup (75 g) chopped green bell pepper

3 garlic cloves, minced

6 Tatuma squash or zucchini, peeled and cut into 1-inch (2.5 cm) pieces

¼ cup (60 ml) Mexican Spice Blend (Especias Mexicanas, page 24)

1½ teaspoons salt

2 tablespoons masa harina

**1.** Heat 1½ teaspoons of the oil in a large skillet over medium heat. Cook the chicken until slightly browned, 7 to 8 minutes. Remove from the skillet and set aside.

**2.** Heat the remaining 1 tablespoon oil in the skillet. Add the tomato, corn, onion, and pepper and sauté until the onion is translucent, about 5 minutes. Add the garlic and sauté for 1 more minute.

**3.** Add the squash, chicken, spice blend, and salt and stir well. Cook until the squash is tender, about 10 minutes.

**4.** Bring to a boil, then reduce the heat and simmer, covered, for 30 minutes, to allow the flavors to blend well.

**5.** Combine the masa harina and 3 tablespoons water in a small bowl. Add to the skillet and stir well. Simmer, uncovered, until the broth thickens slightly, 5 to 10 minutes. Season to taste before serving.

––––––––

Per serving:
CALORIES 185; FAT 7 g (sat 1 g); PROTEIN 21 g; CARB 10 g; FIBER 3 g;
SUGARS 4 g; SODIUM 666 mg

## Tamales de Pollo
# CHICKEN TAMALES
### ←·**Makes about 24 tamales**·→

*For many people of Mexican heritage, the arrival of cooler weather prompts the desire to eat tamales. They are an essential part of traditional Mexican food prepared for Christmas and the New Year.*

*In Mexican American culture, the tamalada is a time when generations gather to help in this traditional food preparation. Experienced grandmothers offer their advice on numerous preparations. Each family has its own heirloom recipe.*

*Making tamales is an ancient tradition, passed down from our indigenous ancestors. Technology has changed considerably from the days when they ground their maize by hand. But this important tradition endures. Each year, we gather to prepare this food, to laugh, talk, and strengthen the weaves of our family ties.*

*This is a simple way to cook tamales—there are methods that are much more complicated. You can also embellish them with different spices or fillings. These tamales should be cooked or frozen within twenty-four hours. They will keep in the freezer for up to six months.*

**MASA (DOUGH)**

1¾ cups (210 g) masa harina

1 tablespoon chili powder

1 teaspoon salt

½ teaspoon baking powder

½ teaspoon garlic powder

1 to 1¼ cups (240 to 300 ml) reduced-sodium chicken or vegetable broth, warmed

1 tablespoon butter/oil blend, such as Land O'Lakes butter with olive oil

½ cup (120 ml) canola oil

**HUSKS**

One 16-ounce (454 g) package dried corn husks

Warm water

**FILLING**

1½ pounds (680 g) boneless, skinless chicken breast, cooked and shredded

2 garlic cloves, minced

¼ cup (60 ml) Mexican Spice Blend (Especias Mexicanas, page 24)

1 teaspoon chili powder

½ teaspoon salt

Boiling water, for steaming

**1.** To prepare the masa, whisk the masa harina, chili powder, salt, baking powder, and garlic powder in a large bowl.

**2.** Combine 1 cup of the broth and butter in a microwave-safe bowl. Microwave until the butter melts, about 30 seconds, then add the oil. Mix well. Add to the bowl with the masa harina and mix by hand for 3 to 4 minutes. The dough should be smooth, with a consistency of moist mashed potatoes. Add the remaining broth as needed. Cover and refrigerate for 2 to 3 hours or overnight.

**3.** To prepare the husks, separate and rinse them to remove corn silk and debris. Fill a large container with very warm water and soak the husks for at least 3 hours, until softened and pliable.

**4.** To prepare the filling, cook the chicken, garlic, spice blend, chili powder, and salt in a medium saucepan over medium heat for 10 minutes, or until most of the liquid evaporates. Remove from the heat and set aside to cool.

**5.** To assemble the tamales, drain the husks and cut each to about 5 x 8 inches (13 x 20 cm) in size. Pat each husk dry and remove any debris.

**6.** Set out the filling, masa, and husks on a large work surface. Hold one husk in the palm of your hand. Spread 1½ to 2 tablespoons of the masa evenly on the bottom 4 inches (10 cm) of the husk (the larger end) with the back of a spoon to about ⅛-inch (3 mm) thick. You may need to pat gently with your fingers to create a smooth surface.

**7.** Spread 1½ to 2 tablespoons of the filling vertically on the middle third of the masa, then carefully roll up the husk from right to left. Gently seal the edge of the tamale with your fingertips, maintaining its round shape. Fold the top part under toward the open part of the tamale. Repeat with the remaining husks, masa, and filling.

**8.** To steam the tamales, set a steamer basket in a large pot with a lid. Arrange the tamales snugly, upright, in the steamer basket, with the opening of each tamale facing upward. Do not overcrowd the pan or the tamales will not cook properly.

**9.** Carefully pour 2 inches (5 cm) boiling water around the edges of the tamales. Do not pour the water into the tamales or allow the water to touch the top of the tamales, as they will become waterlogged. Quickly cover the pot with aluminum foil to form a tight seal. Place the pot lid over the foil.

· · · · · · · · · · · · · · · · · · · · · · · · · **HEALTHY EASY MEXICAN** · · · · · · · · · · · · · · · · · · · · · · · · ·

180

**10.** Simmer over low heat for 45 minutes. Check after 30 minutes to make sure there's still sufficient water for steaming, and add more boiling water around the sides of the tamales if necessary.

**11.** Allow the tamales to cool for at least 15 minutes before serving.

———

Per serving (2 tamales):
CALORIES 218; FAT 11 g (sat 1 g); PROTEIN 15 g; CARB  15 g; FIBER 1 g;
SUGARS 0 g; SODIUM 357 mg

**Tamales de Frijoles con Queso/Bean and Cheese Tamales:** Instead of preparing the chicken filling, use 1½ cups (255 g) cooked pinto beans and twelve 1-ounce (28 g) pieces mozzarella string cheese. Mash the beans, then halve each piece of cheese lengthwise and cut to 3 inches (7.5 cm) in length. Fill each tamale with about 1 tablespoon beans and one strip of cheese, leaving about 1 inch (2.5 cm) from the bottom free of cheese, which will expand.

———

Per serving (2 tamales):
CALORIES 236; FAT 12 g (sat 2 g); PROTEIN 12 g; CARB 21 g; FIBER 3 g;
SUGARS 0 g; SODIUM 443 mg

**Tamales de Chile y Queso/Chile Cheese Tamales:** Instead of preparing the chicken filling, use twenty-four 1-ounce (28 g) pieces mozzarella string cheese and canned long-sliced green chiles (*rajas*). Halve each piece of cheese lengthwise and cut into pieces 3 inches (7.5 cm) long. Fill each tamale with one piece of cheese and two strips of green chile, leaving about 1 inch (2.5 cm) from the bottom free of cheese, which will expand.

———

Per serving (2 tamales):
CALORIES 261; FAT 14 g (sat 3 g); PROTEIN 18 g; CARB 18 g; FIBER 2 g;
SUGARS 1 g; SODIUM 741 mg

## Arroz con Pollo
# MEXICAN CHICKEN AND RICE
### ➤· Serves 6 ·➤

*Arroz con pollo is one of those Mexican comfort foods that is great on a cold winter day. There are many variations, but all are usually served with delicious homemade pinto beans like Frijoles de Olla (page 223). You can use frozen corn instead of peas and carrots, and brown rice instead of white, for a whole grain dish. If using brown rice, increase the broth per package instructions and the simmering time to 40 minutes.*

2 tablespoons olive oil

1½ pounds (680 g) boneless, skinless chicken breasts, chopped into 1.5-inch (4 cm) cubes

1½ cups (300 g) white basmati rice

2 tablespoons finely chopped onion

3 cups (720 ml) low-sodium chicken broth

1 cup (240 g) canned diced tomatoes or diced fire-roasted tomatoes

½ teaspoon salt

¼ cup (60 ml) Mexican Spice Blend (Especias Mexicanas, page 24)

2 garlic cloves, crushed

1 cup (140 g) mixed frozen peas and carrots, thawed

**1.** Heat 1 tablespoon of the oil in a large skillet over medium heat. Add the chicken and cook until browned, 7 to 10 minutes. Remove from the pan and set aside.

**2.** Add the remaining 1 tablespoon oil to the pan. Sauté the rice and onion, stirring frequently, until the rice has turned opaque and a light brown color, about 5 minutes. Add the chicken broth, tomatoes, and salt. Add the spice blend and garlic and bring to a boil, stirring well.

**3.** Arrange the chicken on top of the rice mixture. Cover, reduce the heat to low, and simmer for 20 minutes. Add the peas and carrots, cover, and heat for 5 minutes, until the vegetables are warmed through.

———

Per serving:
CALORIES 379; FAT 7 g (sat 0 g); PROTEIN 31 g; CARB 43 g; FIBER 2 g;
SUGARS 3 g; SODIUM 442 mg

## Tacos de Pavo con Crema Chipotle

# TURKEY TACOS WITH CHIPOTLE-LIME SAUCE

➤· Serves 4 ·⬅

*This is a great way to use turkey leftovers. This sauce, with Greek yogurt, chipotles and lime juice, adds a spicy yet tart flavor to the turkey, and the carrots provide vitamins and fiber. Dial the heat up or down by adding more or less chipotle.*

1 cup (110 g) peeled, shredded carrot

½ cup (120 g) low-fat plain Greek yogurt

2 tablespoons fresh lime juice

½ canned chipotle chile, chopped, plus 1 teaspoon adobo sauce

½ teaspoon salt

¼ teaspoon ground cumin

2 cups (270 g) shredded cooked turkey breast, warmed

1 medium tomato, diced

8 corn tortillas (Tortillas de Maíz, page 105), warmed

2 ounces (55 g) reduced-fat cheddar, grated (½ cup)

Shredded lettuce

**1.** Combine the carrots, yogurt, lime juice, chipotle and adobo, salt, and cumin in a medium bowl. Mix thoroughly. Add the turkey and tomato and toss gently.

**2.** Divide the turkey mixture into 8 equal portions and arrange on the tortillas. Top with the cheese and lettuce.

———

Per serving:
CALORIES 263; FAT 6 g (sat 3 g); PROTEIN 26 g; CARB 27 g; FIBER 4 g;
SUGARS 4 g; SODIUM 738 mg

## Tacos de Pavo con Frijoles y Chile

# TURKEY TACOS WITH CHILES AND BEANS

**←· Serves 4 ·→**

*There's plenty of flavor in these hearty tacos from the onions, cumin, chiles, and tomatoes. Beans enhance the taste and texture. Serve with Crema Chipotle (page 46).*

1 pound (455 g) ground turkey breast

½ cup (60 g) chopped onion

1 garlic clove, minced

1 cup (240 ml) no-salt-added tomato sauce

2 teaspoons chili powder

½ teaspoon ground cumin

¼ teaspoon dried Mexican oregano

1 cup (170 g) cooked pinto beans

½ cup (120 g) drained canned diced green chiles

8 corn tortillas (Tortillas de Maíz, page 105), warmed

½ cup (120 g) low-fat plain Greek yogurt

1 medium tomato, seeded and chopped

Shredded lettuce

**1.** Place the turkey, onion, and garlic in a large nonstick skillet over medium heat. Sauté until the turkey has browned, 8 to 10 minutes.

**2.** Add the tomato sauce, chili powder, cumin, and oregano and simmer for about 15 minutes, until the flavors have blended. Add the beans and chiles and simmer for about 15 minutes more, until the beans are thoroughly warmed.

**3.** Arrange on the tortillas. Top with the yogurt, tomato, and lettuce.

———

Per serving (without lettuce):
CALORIES 344; FAT 4 g (sat 1 g); PROTEIN 38 g; CARB 42 g; FIBER 10 g;
SUGARS 7 g; SODIUM 462 mg

Papas Doradas con Chorizo de Pavo

# PANFRIED POTATOES WITH TURKEY CHORIZO

**• Serves 4 •**

*This recipe makes a great breakfast with a side of fresh fruit and some Tortillas de Maíz (page 105). The potatoes are creamy, and the onions and garlic add even more flavor to the chorizo.*

2 tablespoons olive oil or other vegetable oil, plus more if needed

¼ medium onion, chopped

1 garlic clove, minced

1 cup (145 g) Turkey Chorizo (Chorizo de Pavo, page 188), uncooked

4 medium Yukon Gold potatoes, cut into about 1-inch (2.5 cm) cubes

Chipotle Cream Sauce (Crema Chipotle, page 46; optional)

**1.** Heat 1 tablespoon of the oil in a large skillet over medium heat. Add the onion and sauté until translucent, 5 to 6 minutes. Add the garlic and sauté for 1 more minute. Remove from the skillet and set aside.

**2.** Add the chorizo to the skillet and cook for 5 to 7 minutes, stirring frequently. Remove from the skillet and add to the onion and garlic.

**3.** Heat the remaining 1 tablespoon oil in the skillet and add the potatoes. Toss well, then cover. Cook for 10 to 15 minutes, until the potatoes can be pierced easily with a fork, stirring occasionally, then remove the lid and add a little more oil, if needed. Continue cooking until the potatoes are browned, 5 to 10 minutes.

**4.** Add the chorizo, onion, and garlic and stir to combine. Drizzle with the chipotle cream, if desired, and serve immediately.

———

Per serving:
CALORIES 158; FAT 8 g (sat 1 g); PROTEIN 11 g; CARB 13 g; FIBER 6 g;
SUGARS 2 g; SODIUM 475 mg

## Chorizo de Pavo

# TURKEY CHORIZO

### ➼· Serves 8 ·➼

*Chorizo is a spicy pork sausage, often prepared with eggs, beans, or potatoes and served with tortillas, usually for breakfast tacos. Cooked chorizo can also be added to mashed pinto beans (Frijoles Refritos sin Freir, page 224) to make an awesome dip for Tortillas Doradas (page 107). This recipe is a healthier replacement for regular, higher-fat pork chorizo. Lean ground pork tenderloin, ground chicken, or lean ground beef can be substituted for turkey.*

1 pound (455 g) ground turkey breast

¼ cup (60 ml) white vinegar

2 tablespoons finely chopped onion

1 garlic clove, finely minced

1 tablespoon chili powder

1 tablespoon paprika

1 tablespoon salt

⅛ teaspoon dried Mexican oregano

2 teaspoons olive oil

**1.** Mix the turkey, vinegar, onion, garlic, chili powder, paprika, salt, and oregano in a medium bowl. Cover and refrigerate overnight to allow the flavors to blend. If not using the entire recipe, freeze the remaining chorizo.

**2.** Heat the oil in a medium skillet over medium heat. Add the chorizo and sauté until it is cooked through and reaches a temperature of 160°F (70°C), 8 to 10 minutes.

———

Per serving:
CALORIES 78; FAT 2 g (sat 0 g); PROTEIN 14 g; CARB 1 g; FIBER 1 g;
SUGARS 0 g; SODIUM 920 mg

Fideo con Pavo

# TURKEY VERMICELLI

**━·• Serves 6 •·━**

*This is a great recipe for using turkey leftovers after the holidays and can be prepared in under half an hour. Serve with Frijoles de Olla (page 223) and a simple green salad for an easy weeknight dinner.*

1 tablespoon olive oil

10 ounces (280 g) vermicelli, broken into 2-inch (5 cm) pieces

¼ cup (35 g) chopped green bell pepper

½ cup (60 g) chopped onion

3 garlic cloves, minced

2¼ cups (300 g) chopped cooked turkey breast

4 cups (960 ml) hot water

½ cup (20 g) chopped cilantro

¼ cup (60 ml) no-salt-added tomato sauce

2 tablespoons chili powder

2 teaspoons Mexican Spice Blend (Especias Mexicanas, page 24)

½ teaspoon salt

**1.** Heat the oil in a large skillet over medium heat and add the vermicelli. Cook until lightly browned, 2 to 3 minutes. Add the pepper, onion, and garlic and sauté until the vermicelli is golden brown, about 7 minutes. Watch carefully, as the vermicelli burns easily.

**2.** Add the turkey, hot water, cilantro, tomato sauce, chili powder, spice blend, and salt and bring to a boil. Reduce the heat, cover, and simmer for about 15 minutes, stirring occasionally, until the vermicelli is tender.

————

Per serving:
CALORIES 260; FAT 8 g (sat 1 g); PROTEIN 21 g; CARB 31 g; FIBER 3 g;
SUGARS 2 g; SODIUM 276 mg

Tacos de Camote
## SWEET POTATO TACOS
195

Huevos Rancheros Horneados
## BAKED HUEVOS RANCHEROS
196

Tostadas de Frijol y Queso
## CORN TOSTADAS WITH BEANS
## AND CHEESE
198

Enchiladas de Chile Colorado
## RED CHILE CHEESE ENCHILADAS
199

Entomatadas
## ENCHILADAS IN SPICY TOMATO SAUCE
200

Enchiladas de Hongos y Queso
## MUSHROOM AND CHEESE ENCHILADAS
202

Tortas con Frijoles y Queso
## BEAN AND CHEESE TORTAS
205

Calabaza con Queso Panela
## TATUMA SQUASH WITH PANELA CHEESE
206

Albóndigas de Elote
## CORN CAKES
207

COMIDAS
SIN CARNE

# MEATLESS
# MEALS

**M**ake vegetables the star of the show! There are just so many reasons to love them. They are rich in vitamins and fiber, and eating more of them is one way to help prevent cancer. I keep vegetables such as carrots, cabbage, and spinach on hand—they're nutritious and keep well in the refrigerator. Many meatless meals, such as those in this chapter, can be prepared using combinations of grains and vegetables.

## Tacos de Camote
# SWEET POTATO TACOS
### ⊷· Serves 4 ·⊶

*Sweet potatoes are nutritional superstars: They're rich in vitamin A, fiber, and potassium. Sautéed lightly, caramelized, and tucked away in a corn tortilla topped with a bit of queso fresco and cilantro, they make a fabulous meat-free taco. For more visual interest, prepare these with blue corn tortillas. Serve with Ensalada de Coditos con Cilantro (page 125).*

3 medium sweet potatoes

3 tablespoons butter/oil blend, such as Land O'Lakes butter with olive oil

½ teaspoon salt

½ teaspoon black pepper

8 corn tortillas (Tortillas de Maíz, page 105)

½ cup (60 g) crumbled queso fresco

½ cup (20 g) finely chopped cilantro

Pickled jalapeños (optional)

Scallions (optional)

**1.** Fill a large saucepan with water, add the sweet potatoes, and boil until they are cooked al dente, 20 to 35 minutes. Remove the potatoes and let cool.

**2.** Peel the potatoes and cut into ¼-inch (6 mm) slices.

**3.** Heat the butter in a large, heavy skillet over medium-high heat. Add the potato slices, season with the salt and pepper, and sauté, turning occasionally, until slightly caramelized, about 10 minutes.

**4.** Warm the tortillas. Place two or three sweet potato rounds on each tortilla. Garnish with the queso fresco and cilantro along with jalapeños, and scallions, if desired.

———

Per serving:
CALORIES 315; FAT 12 g (sat 5 g); PROTEIN 8 g; CARB 46 g; FIBER 6 g;
SUGARS 6 g; SODIUM 642 mg

Huevos Rancheros Horneados

# BAKED HUEVOS RANCHEROS

➤· Serves 4 ·➤

*Typically, huevos rancheros are made with fried eggs, fried tortillas, and refried beans. These are much lower in calories and so simple to prepare. Make them with Salsa Ranchera (page 33) or a salsa of your choosing. Eggs are a great source of protein, eaten in moderation. Serve with a side of fresh fruit for a delightful breakfast.*

3 cups (720 ml) Ranchero Sauce (Salsa Ranchera, page 33) or other salsa

½ cup (70 g) frozen corn kernels, thawed

4 eggs

1 cup (260 g) Unfried Refried Beans (Frijoles Refritos sin Freir, page 224)

8 corn tortillas (Tortillas de Maíz, page 105)

Chopped cilantro (optional)

**1.** Preheat the oven to 375°F (190°C).

**2.** Combine the salsa and corn in an 8 x 8-inch (20 x 20 cm) ovenproof dish and create 4 indentations with the back of a spoon. Crack the eggs into each indentation. Bake for 20 minutes, or until the whites are just set and the yolks are still runny.

**3.** While the eggs are baking, warm the beans and tortillas. Place the tortillas on a baking sheet and spread each one with 2 tablespoons of the beans.

**4.** Place two tortillas to overlap on a serving plate and add a baked egg on top. Cover with salsa from the baking dish, sprinkle with cilantro, if desired, and serve.

---

Per serving:<br>
CALORIES 289; FAT 8 g (sat 2 g); PROTEIN 14 g; CARB 43 g; FIBER 9 g;<br>
SUGARS 7 g; SODIUM 755 mg

## Tostadas de Frijol y Queso
# CORN TOSTADAS WITH BEANS AND CHEESE
### ⭠• Serves 6 •⭢

*Keeping a few simple ingredients on hand can make for a very easy meatless, gluten-free meal. If you don't have time to make the tostadas yourself, you can find many good baked options at the grocery store. I absolutely love having these for a quick weeknight meal using pinto beans made in a slow cooker. Try this recipe using Frijoles Negros (page 225).*

12 corn tortillas (Tortillas de Maíz, page 105)

1 tablespoon olive oil

1 recipe Unfried Refried Beans (Frijoles Refritos sin Freir, page 224), warmed

2 ounces (55 g) reduced-fat Monterey Jack, grated (½ cup)

2 ounces (55 g) reduced-fat cheddar, grated (½ cup)

1 cup (70 g) shredded iceberg lettuce

2 Roma tomatoes, cored, seeded, and finely chopped

3 scallions, chopped

**1.** Preheat the oven to 400°F (200°C).

**2.** Place the tortillas on a baking sheet. Brush both sides lightly with the oil. Bake for 5 minutes, checking often to make sure the tortillas do not burn.

**3.** Remove from the oven and flip the tortillas over to allow for even baking. Return to the oven and bake for 3 to 4 minutes, until crisp. Remove from the oven and reduce the heat to 350°F (180°C).

**4.** Spread the beans on the baked tortillas and top with the cheeses. Bake for 3 to 4 minutes, until the cheese melts. Top with the lettuce, tomatoes, and scallions and serve.

---

Per serving:
CALORIES 298; FAT 8 g (sat 3 g); PROTEIN 15 g; CARB 45 g; FIBER 11 g; SUGARS 3 g; SODIUM 624 mg

## Enchiladas de Chile Colorado

# RED CHILE CHEESE ENCHILADAS

### ← · Serves 6 · →

*These enchiladas are probably the most common Mexican dish. The typical enchilada begins with a fried tortilla that is filled with cheese, but it's high in saturated fat. In this recipe, I've reduced the calories and saturated fat content by steaming the tortillas and using a lower-fat cheese. Want to make this recipe even simpler? Substitute a slice of good-quality reduced-fat cheese in the tortilla—this saves you the step of grating cheese. Experiment with any reduced-fat cheese you like.*

12 corn tortillas (store-bought is best)

3 cups (720 ml) Red Chile Sauce (Salsa de Chile Colorado, page 36)

12 ounces (335 g) reduced-fat cheddar, grated (3 cups)

½ cup (80 g) finely chopped onion

**1.** Preheat the oven to 350°F (180°C).

**2.** Place the tortillas, six at a time, between clean damp kitchen towels and microwave for 1 minute, or until softened.

**3.** Pour about ½ cup (120 ml) of the red chile sauce in the bottom of a baking dish. Spread evenly.

**4.** Lay a tortilla flat on a plate or cutting board and place 3 tablespoons of the cheddar and 2 teaspoons of the onion in the center. Roll the tortilla, then place it seam side down in the baking dish. Repeat with the remaining tortillas, reserving ½ cup (55 g) of the cheese, then pour the remaining sauce over the top, making sure the sauce gets between each enchilada.

**5.** Bake for 10 minutes, then remove from the oven and top with the remaining cheese. Bake for 10 minutes more, or until the sauce begins to bubble slightly and the cheese is melted.

———

Per serving:
CALORIES 421; FAT 23 g (sat 8 g); PROTEIN 18 g; CARB 34 g; FIBER 5 g;
SUGARS 1 g; SODIUM 795 mg

· · · · · · · · · · · · · · · · · · · · · · · · · · **MEATLESS MEALS** · · · · · · · · · · · · · · · · · · · · · · · · · ·

199

Entomatadas

# ENCHILADAS IN SPICY TOMATO SAUCE

**◄•· Serves 4 ·►**

*In Mexico, entomatadas are typically served for breakfast, but this is a great meatless meal that can be served any time of the day. The roasted tomato sauce is simmered to bring out all of the delicious flavors. Serve with sliced avocado and beans, like Frijoles Negros (page 225).*

Nonstick cooking spray

5 medium tomatoes

½ medium yellow onion, separated into layers

2 garlic cloves, minced

2 tablespoons Mexican Spice Blend (Especias Mexicanas, page 24)

8 corn tortillas (store-bought is best)

10 ounces (280 g) reduced-fat Monterey Jack, grated (2½ cups)

Chopped cilantro

**1.** Preheat the oven to 350°F (180°C). Spray a 9-inch (23 cm) square baking dish with cooking spray.

**2.** Place the tomatoes and onion in a large, heavy dry skillet over medium-high heat. Roast until brown patches appear, 20 to 25 minutes, stirring often to make sure all parts char equally but do not burn. Add the garlic and sauté for 1 additional minute, until fragrant.

**3.** Let cool slightly, then transfer to a blender. Remove the blender lid's center insert and cover the opening with a clean kitchen towel. Blend until most of the large pieces are pureed, leaving some for texture.

**4.** Pour the sauce back into the skillet, then add the spice blend. Bring to a boil, cover, and simmer gently for 10 to 15 minutes to allow the flavors to blend well.

**5.** Pour ¼ cup (60 ml) of the sauce into the bottom of the baking dish. Spread evenly.

· · · · · · · · · · · · · · · · · · · · · · · · **HEALTHY EASY MEXICAN** · · · · · · · · · · · · · · · · · · · · · · · ·

200

**6.** Place the tortillas, four at a time, between clean damp kitchen towels, and microwave for about 1 minute, until softened.

**7.** Lay a tortilla flat on a plate or cutting board and place 3 tablespoons of the cheese in the center. Roll the tortilla, then place it seam side down in the baking dish. Repeat with the remaining tortillas, then pour the remaining sauce over the top, making sure the sauce gets between each entomatada.

**8.** Bake for 10 minutes, then remove from the oven and top with the remaining cheese. Bake for 10 minutes more, or until the cheese is melted. Serve warm, topped with cilantro, if desired.

———

Per serving:
CALORIES 357; FAT 17 g (sat 10 g); PROTEIN 22 g; CARB 33 g; FIBER 5 g;
SUGARS 5 g; SODIUM 698 mg

## Enchiladas de Hongos y Queso
# MUSHROOM AND CHEESE ENCHILADAS
### ━•· Serves 6 ·•━

*Mushroom enchiladas are certainly a twist on conventional cheese or beef enchiladas. The mushrooms make them a great lower-fat option. Served with Calabaza con Queso Panela (page 206) and sliced jicama, this makes a tasty vegetarian meal.*

Nonstick cooking spray

1 tablespoon olive oil

1½ pounds (680 g) white mushrooms, chopped

12 corn tortillas (store-bought is best)

3 cups (720 ml) Red Chile Sauce (Salsa de Chile Colorado, page 36) or Ancho Chile Sauce (Salsa de Chile Ancho, page 38)

4 ounces (115 g) reduced-fat Monterey Jack, grated (1 cup

**1.** Preheat the oven to 350°F (180°C).

**2.** Heat the oil in a large skillet over medium heat, then add the mushrooms and sauté until tender, 5 to 7 minutes.

**3.** Place the tortillas, six at a time, between clean damp kitchen towels, and microwave for about 1 minute, until softened.

**4.** Pour about ½ cup (120 ml) chile sauce to coat the bottom of a 9 x 13-inch (23 x 33 cm) baking dish. Spread evenly.

**5.** Dip a tortilla in the remaining sauce until well coated on both sides. Lay the tortilla flat on a plate or cutting board and place 1 teaspoon of the cheese and about 2 tablespoons of the mushrooms in the center. Roll the tortilla, then place it seam side down in the baking dish. Repeat with the remaining tortillas, then pour the remaining sauce over the top, making sure the sauce gets between each enchilada.

**5.** Bake for 10 minutes, then remove from the oven and top with the remaining cheese. Bake for 5 to 10 minutes, or until the sauce begins to bubble slightly and the cheese is melted.

———

Per serving:
CALORIES 340; FAT 18 g (sat 3 g); PROTEIN 12 g; CARB 37 g; FIBER 6 g; SUGARS 2 g; SODIUM 485 mg

## Tortas con Frijoles y Queso
# BEAN AND CHEESE TORTAS
➤· Serves 6 ·➤

*This recipe takes simple ingredients and elevates them into a satisfying meal. This traditional breakfast dish is usually made with bolillos—crusty bread rolls. Garnish with Salsa de Tomatillo Tatemado (page 44) or top with diced avocado and tomatoes.*

2 cups (520 g) Unfried Refried Beans (Frijoles Refritos sin Freir, page 224), warmed

6 Mexican Rolls (Bolillos, page 101), sliced horizontally and toasted, or ½ loaf French bread, cut into 12 slices and toasted

2 ounces (55 g) reduced-fat Monterey Jack, grated (½ cup)

2 ounces (55 g) reduced-fat cheddar, grated (½ cup)

Ranchero Sauce (Salsa Ranchera, page 33)

**1.** Preheat the oven to 350°F (180°C).

**2.** Spread the beans on one side of each slice of the toasted bread, then place on a baking sheet. Mix the cheeses in a small bowl, then sprinkle on top of the beans.

**3.** Bake until the cheese has melted, 5 to 7 minutes. Serve with the salsa.

———

Per serving (without salsa):
CALORIES 292; FAT 6 g (sat 4 g); PROTEIN 13 g; CARB 45 g; FIBER 6 g;
SUGARS 3 g; SODIUM 730 mg

## Calabaza con Queso Panela

# TATUMA SQUASH WITH PANELA CHEESE

**━·• Serves 5 •·━**

*Tatuma squash makes a wonderful meatless meal when combined with panela, a reduced-fat Mexican cheese. The squash, which is similar to zucchini, has very delicate seeds that need not be removed before preparing. This is a filling one-pot meal when accompanied by warm Tortillas de Maíz (page 105).*

2 Roma tomatoes, chopped

2 garlic cloves

½ teaspoon salt

1 tablespoon olive oil

½ yellow onion, finely chopped

¼ cup (60 ml) Mexican Spice Blend (Especias Mexicanas, page 24)

4 medium Tatuma squash or zucchini, cut into 1½-inch (4 cm) cubes

½ cup (70 g) frozen corn kernels, thawed

½ cup (20 g) chopped cilantro

4 ounces (115 g) part-skim panela cheese, cubed

**1.** Place the tomatoes, garlic, salt, and ¼ cup (60 ml) water in a blender. Blend to form a chunky sauce.

**2.** Heat the oil in a large skillet over medium heat and sauté the onion until translucent, 5 to 6 minutes. Add the tomato sauce and spice blend and warm through.

**3.** Add the squash and corn and stir to combine. Bring to a boil, cover, and simmer gently for about 10 minutes, stirring occasionally, until the squash is tender. Add the cilantro and cheese and stir until the cheese is slightly warmed, about 5 minutes.

———

Per serving:
CALORIES 137; FAT 8 g (sat 4 g); PROTEIN 8 g; CARB 9 g; FIBER 3 g;
SUGARS 5 g; SODIUM 357 mg

· · · · · · · · · · · · · · · · · · · · · · · ·• **HEALTHY EASY MEXICAN** •· · · · · · · · · · · · · · · · · · · · · · · ·

206

# Albóndigas de Elote
# CORN CAKES

### ← · Serves 5 · →

*This recipe dates back to 1899—it's been passed down through the generations of my husband's family, who were a ranching family in the early Texas days. It's representative of the way our ancestors prepared meals—with simple, wholesome, homegrown ingredients. But I've added a few things, like green chiles and cheddar cheese, to make this recipe a bit more interesting. Serve with Crema Chipotle (page 46) for a quick weekend lunch.*

2 tablespoons flour

¼ teaspoon salt

¼ teaspoon black pepper

4 ears corn, kernels removed, or 2½ cups (340 g) frozen corn kernels, thawed

½ cup (120 g) drained canned diced green chiles

2 ounces (55 g) reduced-fat sharp cheddar, grated (½ cup)

2 eggs, whites and yolks separated

¼ cup (60 ml) olive oil

**1.** Whisk together the flour, salt, and pepper in a large bowl. Add the corn, chiles, and cheddar and stir to combine.

**2.** In a separate large bowl, beat the egg whites for about 45 seconds, or until no longer frothy.

**3.** Beat the egg yolks in a separate bowl, then slowly fold them into the egg whites. Fold in the corn mixture.

**4.** Heat the oil in a large skillet over medium heat. Add the corn cake batter in 1-tablespoon dollops. Cook for about 2 minutes on each side, or until golden brown. Drain on paper towels before serving.

———

Per serving:
CALORIES 181; FAT 11 g (sat 3 g); PROTEIN 7 g; CARB 14 g; FIBER 2 g;
SUGARS 5 g; SODIUM 304 mg

## ARROZ ~ RICE

Arroz Mexicano
### MEXICAN RICE
213

Arroz Blanco con Elote y Cebolla
### RICE WITH CORN AND ONIONS
214

Arroz con Comino
### CUMIN RICE
215

Arroz con Crema y Chile Poblano
### CREAMY RICE WITH POBLANO CHILE
216

Arroz con Calabacita
### BROWN RICE WITH ZUCCHINI
218

Arroz con Jalapeños
### JALAPEÑO RICE
219

Arroz con Ajo y Lima
### GARLIC-LIME RICE
220

Arroz con Camarón Seco
### MEXICAN RICE WITH SHRIMP
221

Arroz Suroeste
### SOUTHWESTERN RICE CASSEROLE
222

## FRIJOLES ~ BEANS

Frijoles de Olla
### MEXICAN-STYLE PINTO BEANS
223

Frijoles Refritos sin Freir
### UNFRIED REFRIED BEANS
224

Frijoles Negros
### BLACK BEANS
225

# ARROZ Y FRIJOLES

# RICE & BEANS

The simple bean, whether it be the pinto bean, the kidney bean, or the black bean, has risen in popularity, because it is a tiny yet powerful nutrition source. Beans are rich in protein, iron, potassium, and fiber. And they're economical as well as shelf-stable. Stored in an airtight container, they can keep for months. Beans can be prepared in a myriad of ways. Once prepared, they freeze well.

Combining beans and rice is an excellent way to make a complete, delicious meal. One of the best comfort meals is a bowl of savory beans ladled over a bed of steaming rice. All of my rice recipes can be made using brown rice, which is richer in nutrients and fiber than white rice.

# Arroz Mexicano

# MEXICAN RICE

**⟶· Serves 6 ·⟵**

*Pair this with some fresh Frijoles de Olla (page 223) and you have a complete meal. To prepare this using brown rice, increase the broth per package instructions and the simmering time to 50 minutes. This can also be made with cauliflower rice!*

1 cup (200 g) white basmati rice

1¾ cups (420 ml) hot water

3 tablespoons fresh lemon juice

1 tablespoon olive or canola oil

2 medium tomatoes, seeded and chopped

½ medium green bell pepper, chopped

2 garlic cloves, crushed

¼ cup (60 ml) Mexican Spice Blend (Especias Mexicanas, page 24)

2 cups (480 ml) low-sodium chicken or vegetable broth

¼ cup (10 g) chopped cilantro

**1.** Cover the rice with the hot water in a large bowl. Add the lemon juice and soak for 5 minutes. Drain.

**2.** Heat the oil in large nonstick skillet over medium heat. Add the rice and sauté until lightly brown, about 5 minutes. Stir in the tomatoes, pepper, garlic, and spice blend.

**3.** Add the broth and cilantro and bring to a boil. Cover, reduce the heat to low, and simmer for 20 minutes, or until all the liquid is absorbed. Fluff the rice before serving.

———

Per serving:
CALORIES 169; FAT 3 g (sat 0 g); PROTEIN 3 g; CARB 30 g; FIBER 1 g;
SUGARS 2 g; SODIUM 37 mg

## Arroz Blanco con Elote y Cebolla
# RICE WITH CORN AND ONIONS
### ← · Serves 7 · →

*This rice, a family favorite, gets its wonderful flavor from the addition of garlic, corn, and bay leaves. I like to prepare it in advance and freeze it, because it makes a fabulous dish for entertaining. To make this with brown rice, increase the water per package instructions and the simmering time to 50 minutes. Roast the corn beforehand to make the rice even more flavorful!*

3 tablespoons olive oil

½ onion, finely diced

3 garlic cloves, minced

1¼ cups (250 g) white basmati rice, rinsed and drained

1 cup (135 g) frozen corn kernels

2 bay leaves

1 tablespoon butter/oil blend, such as Land O'Lakes butter with olive oil

1 teaspoon salt

**1.** Heat 1 tablespoon of the oil in a medium skillet over medium heat. Add the onion and sauté until translucent, 5 to 6 minutes. Add the garlic and sauté until fragrant, 1 to 2 minutes. Remove from the pan and set aside.

**2.** Heat the remaining 2 tablespoons oil in the skillet, then add the rice and sauté until it turns opaque, 7 to 10 minutes. Return the onion and garlic to the pan, then add the corn.

**3.** Add 2½ cups (600 ml) water, the bay leaves, butter, and salt and stir well. Bring to a boil, cover, reduce the heat to low, and cook for about 20 minutes, until the liquid is absorbed and the rice is tender. Remove the bay leaves and fluff before serving.

———

Per serving:
CALORIES 218; FAT 8 g (sat 1 g); PROTEIN 3 g; CARB 32 g; FIBER 1 g;
SUGARS 2 g; SODIUM 346 mg

## Arroz con Comino
# CUMIN RICE
### ← · Serves 6 · →

*Brown rice is healthier than white because it has important nutrients such as iron, manganese, protein, and fiber. This flavorful recipe incorporates peppers, onions, and Mexican spices. Serve it alongside Enchiladas Suizas (page 174).*

1 tablespoon extra virgin olive or canola oil

½ cup (60 g) chopped onion

½ cup (75 g) chopped green bell pepper

¼ cup (35 g) chopped red bell pepper

2 garlic cloves, minced or ground in molcajete

1 teaspoon ground cumin

1 cup (180 g) brown rice

2½ cups (600 ml) low-sodium chicken or vegetable broth, hot

**1.** Heat the oil in a large skillet over medium heat. Sauté the onion and peppers until the onion is translucent, 5 to 6 minutes. Add the garlic, cumin, and rice and stir to combine.

**2.** Add the hot broth and bring to a boil. Reduce the heat to low, cover, and simmer for 45 minutes, or until the rice is tender. Fluff and serve.

———

Per serving:
CALORIES 151; FAT 4 g (sat 1 g); PROTEIN 3 g; CARB 26 g; FIBER 2 g;
SUGARS 1 g; SODIUM 43 mg

## Arroz con Crema y Chile Poblano
# CREAMY RICE WITH POBLANO CHILE

**⊷· Serves 8 ·⊷**

*The addition of yogurt makes this recipe creamy and delicious. To substitute brown rice, increase the broth per package instructions and the simmering time to 50 minutes.*

1 poblano chile

2 tablespoons olive oil

1½ cups (300 g) white basmati rice

½ cup (80 g) finely chopped onion

2 garlic cloves, minced

3 cups (720 ml) reduced-sodium chicken or vegetable broth

2 cups (490 g) low-fat plain yogurt, at room temperature

**1.** Preheat the oven to 400°F (200°C).

**2.** Place the chile on a baking sheet and roast for 20 minutes. Flip the chile and roast on the other side for 20 more minutes, or until the skin is charred.

**3.** Place the pepper in a plastic bag and let sit for 5 to 10 minutes to sweat, then carefully remove the skin, stem, and seeds. Chop roughly.

**4.** Heat the oil in a medium saucepan over medium-low heat. Sauté the onion until translucent, about 5 minutes. Add the garlic and sauté until fragrant, about 1 minute. Remove from the pan.

**5.** Sauté the rice in the pan until opaque, about 5 minutes. Add the broth and bring to a boil; cover, lower the heat, and simmer for 20 minutes, or until the rice is tender. Remove from the heat. Add the chopped chiles and yogurt and mix well. Serve warm.

––––––––

Per serving:
CALORIES 213; FAT 4 g (sat 1 g); PROTEIN 5 g; CARB 35 g; FIBER 1 g; SUGARS 4 g; SODIUM 74 mg

## Arroz con Calabacita

# BROWN RICE WITH ZUCCHINI

### ← · Serves 6 · →

*Adding zucchini, scallions, and cilantro perks up the flavor of this brown rice and makes it richer in nutrients. Zucchini is a great source of potassium and vitamin C. Serve this rice with Albóndigas de Salmón (page 152).*

1 cup (180 g) brown rice

½ teaspoon salt

1 medium zucchini, grated

¼ cup (25 g) finely chopped scallions

2 tablespoons chopped cilantro

**1.** Bring 2½ cups (600 ml) water to a boil in a saucepan. Add the rice and salt and bring to a boil again. Cover, reduce the heat, and simmer for 40 minutes.

**2.** Uncover and add the zucchini, scallions, and cilantro. Cover and steam until the rice is cooked thoroughly, 5 to 10 mintues. Allow to sit for 5 minutes before serving.

———

Per serving:
CALORIES 117; FAT 1 g (sat 0 g); PROTEIN 3 g; CARB 24 g; FIBER 2 g;
SUGARS 1 g; SODIUM 198 mg

· · · · · · · · · · · · · · · · · · · · · · · · · · · **HEALTHY EASY MEXICAN** · · · · · · · · · · · · · · · · · · · · · · · · · ·

218

## Arroz con Jalapeños
# JALAPEÑO RICE
### ← · Serves 6 · →

*Adding jalapeños and celery to basmati rice makes this rice dish interesting. Serve with Carne Guisada (page 144) or Pollo Naranja en Olla de Cocción Lenta (page 169).*

1 tablespoon olive or canola oil

½ cup (60 g) chopped celery

1 tablespoon chopped canned jalapeños

1 cup (200 g) white basmati rice

2 cups (480 ml) low-sodium chicken or vegetable broth

½ teaspoon ground cumin

**1.** Heat the oil in a large skillet over medium heat. Sauté the celery and jalapeños until the celery has softened, 5 to 6 minutes. Remove from the skillet.

**2.** Sauté the rice in the skillet over low heat until it has turned opaque and slightly brown, about 5 minutes.

**3.** Add the broth, cumin, celery, and jalapeños and bring to a boil. Reduce the heat, cover tightly, and steam for 20 minutes, or until the rice is tender. Fluff before serving.

———

Per serving:
CALORIES 154; FAT 3 g (sat 0 g); PROTEIN 3 g; CARB 27 g; FIBER 1 g;
SUGARS 0 g; SODIUM 51 mg

## Arroz con Ajo y Lima
# GARLIC-LIME RICE
### ➤· Serves 6 ·➤

*This rice is super simple to prepare with ingredients you already have on hand. The lime zest and juice add just the right pop of flavor. Make this recipe with brown rice by increasing the water per package instructions and the simmering time to 50 minutes.*

1 large garlic clove, minced

½ teaspoon grated lime zest

¼ cup (60 ml) fresh lime juice

¼ teaspoon salt

1 cup (200 g) white basmati rice

**1.** Bring 2 cups (480 ml) water to a boil in a medium saucepan with the garlic, lime zest, 2 tablespoons of the lime juice, and the salt. Add the rice and allow to come to a boil again.

**2.** Cover tightly, reduce the heat to low, and simmer for 20 minutes, or until the rice is tender. Toss gently with the remaining 2 tablespoons lime juice before serving.

———

Per serving:
CALORIES 129; FAT 0 g (sat 0 g); PROTEIN 2 g; CARB 28 g; FIBER 1 g;
SUGARS 0 g; SODIUM 97 mg

## Arroz con Camarón Seco
# MEXICAN RICE WITH SHRIMP

**← · Serves 6 · →**

*This typical Mexican rice dish incorporates dried shrimp, which gives it a distinct seafood flavor. Make this recipe with brown rice by increasing the water per package instructions and the simmering time to 50 minutes.*

1 cup (200 g) white basmati rice

2 tablespoons diced tomatoes

½ ounce (15 g) dried shrimp (about ⅓ cup), plus more as desired

½ teaspoon salt

**1.** Bring 2 cups (480 ml) water to a boil in a medium saucepan. Add the rice, tomatoes, shrimp, and salt. Allow to come to a boil again.

**2.** Cover, reduce the heat to low, and simmer for 20 minutes, or until the rice is tender. Fluff before serving.

———

Per serving:
CALORIES 134; FAT 0 g (sat 0 g); PROTEIN 4 g; CARB 27 g; FIBER 1 g;
SUGARS 0 g; SODIUM 239 mg

· · · · · · · · · · · · · · · · · · · · · · · · · ·**RICE & BEANS**· · · · · · · · · · · · · · · · · · · · · · · · · · ·

221

## Arroz Suroeste
# SOUTHWESTERN RICE CASSEROLE

**➤· Serves 6 ·➤**

*This is a simple way to prepare brown rice. The chiles and sharp cheese deliver so much flavor! You can add leftover chicken to make a hearty meal.*

Nonstick cooking spray

½ teaspoon salt

1 cup (180 g) brown rice

Scant 1 cup (225 g) low-fat plain yogurt

½ cup (120 g) drained canned diced green chiles

4 ounces (115 g) sharp cheddar, grated (1 cup)

**1.** Preheat the oven to 350°F (180°C). Spray a small casserole dish with cooking spray.

**2.** Pour 2½ cups (600 ml) water and the salt into a saucepan and bring to a boil. Stir in the rice and bring to a boil again; reduce the heat to low and cover. Simmer for 45 to 50 minutes, until the rice is tender. Allow to stand, covered, for 5 minutes, then uncover and let cool slightly.

**3.** Add the yogurt and chiles and mix well. Pour the mixture into the casserole dish, sprinkle with the cheese, and bake for 20 minutes, or until the rice is warmed through and the cheese has melted.

———

Per serving:
CALORIES 215; FAT 8 g (sat 5 g); PROTEIN 8 g; CARB 26 g; FIBER 1 g;
SUGARS 3 g; SODIUM 399 mg

## Frijoles de Olla
# MEXICAN-STYLE PINTO BEANS
### ← · Serves 10 · →

*Traditionally, Mexican beans were prepared in ollas, earthenware pots. Today, we cook them in slow cookers or Dutch ovens. This recipe is a family favorite because it has tons of flavor. I like keeping individual slices of rolled-up bacon in the freezer for easy use. To test your beans for doneness, blow on a spoonful. If the outer part of the bean peels away, they're done! Always start with the freshest dried pinto beans for the best results; when buying them, look for ones that are lighter in color.*

2 cups (390 g) dried pinto beans, picked through, rinsed and drained

2 quarts (2 L) boiling water

2 carrots, peeled and cut into 2-inch (5 cm) pieces

2 garlic cloves, crushed

1 strip bacon, chopped (optional)

1 tablespoon olive oil

1 medium tomato, diced

1 small onion, diced

½ cup (75 g) chopped green bell pepper

½ cup (20 g) chopped cilantro

5 dashes Worcestershire sauce

1 teaspoon chili powder, plus more if desired

1 teaspoon salt

**1.** Place the beans, boiling water, carrots, garlic, bacon, and oil in a slow cooker and stir well. Cover with aluminum foil and top with the lid. Cook on high for 4 to 6 hours, stirring two or three times during the first hour and once per hour after that. Test the beans for doneness after 4 hours.

**2.** When the beans are close to being done, add the tomato, onion, pepper, cilantro, Worcestershire sauce, chili powder, and salt. Stir gently and continue cooking for 30 minutes, or until the beans are done.

———

Per serving (without bacon):
CALORIES 159; FAT 2 g (sat 0 g); PROTEIN 7 g; CARB 28 g; FIBER 10 g;
SUGARS 4 g; SODIUM 247 mg

## Frijoles Refritos sin Freir

# UNFRIED REFRIED BEANS

**Serves 6**

*To make thick, rich "refried" beans, try this method. It has lots of flavor without the addition of oil or the more traditional lard. Use these beans to make Tostadas de Frijol y Queso (page 198), Nachos con Frijoles, Queso y Aguacate (page 62), and Huevos Rancheros Horneados (page 196).*

**3 cups (510 g) cooked pinto beans, 1 cup (240 ml) cooking liquid reserved**

**1.** Heat the beans in a large nonstick skillet over low heat. Use a potato masher to mash the beans to your desired consistency.

**2.** Heat until most of the liquid has evaporated, 10 to 15 minutes, taking care to not allow the beans to become too dry. If they become dry, add a little of the reserved cooking liquid.

Per serving (with beans cooked with salt):
CALORIES 117; FAT 0.5 g (sat 0 g); PROTEIN 7 g; CARB 22 g; FIBER 7 g; SUGARS 2 g; SODIUM 203 mg

## Frijoles Negros
# BLACK BEANS
### ➤• Serves 12 •➤

*Beans are rich in iron, protein, potassium, and fiber. I love cooking these beans and serving them over a bowl of warm Arroz con Comino (page 215). Adding the cilantro and lime juice to the finished beans makes them even more flavorful.*

1 pound (455 g) dried black beans, picked over, rinsed, soaked overnight, and drained

1 green bell pepper, stemmed, seeded, and diced

6 garlic cloves, minced

2 bay leaves

1 teaspoon salt

⅛ teaspoon baking soda

1 strip bacon, chopped (optional)

2 tablespoons olive oil

1 onion, finely chopped

1½ teaspoons ground cumin

1 teaspoon dried oregano

½ cup (20 g) cilantro, finely chopped

Fresh lime juice

**1.** Place the beans in a Dutch oven or large pot, then add water to cover them by 2 inches (5 cm). Add half of the pepper, two of the garlic cloves, the bay leaves, salt, baking soda, and bacon, if using.

**2.** Bring to a boil, then reduce the heat and allow the beans to simmer, partially covered, for 1½ to 2 hours, until tender. Remove from the heat and discard the bay leaves.

**3.** Heat the oil in a large skillet over medium heat. Add the onion and remaining pepper and sauté until the onion is translucent, 5 to 6 minutes. Add the remaining garlic and sauté for 1 minute. Add the cumin and oregano and sauté for 1 minute.

**4.** Add 1 cup (170 g) of the cooked beans and about 2 cups (480 ml) of the cooking liquid to the skillet. Mash the beans with a potato masher until smooth.

**5.** If the beans in the pot seem very watery, remove excess liquid to reach your desired consistency (keeping in mind that the mashed beans will be returned to the pot and cooked a little longer).

**6.** Transfer the mashed beans and vegetables to the pot and simmer until the beans have thickened.

**7.** Just before serving, top with the cilantro and fresh lime juice to taste.

––––––

Per serving (without bacon):
CALORIES 159; FAT 3 g (sat 0 g); PROTEIN 9 g; CARB 26 g; FIBER 6 g;
SUGARS 3 g; SODIUM 210 mg

# POSTRES

# DESSERTS

When I stayed with my abuelita as a child, there was a tradition to stop the housework in the midafternoon and enjoy a cup of coffee or cinnamon tea with sweet Mexican pastries.

The merienda was a time to stop and nourish the body, but it was also a time to soothe the spirit and enjoy family or friends. The pace of the day was slowed for enough time to stop and relish the warmth of good food and good company.

The thought of the meriendas at my grandmother's evokes memories of the smell of strong coffee brewed in an aluminum stovetop coffeepot and sweet scents coming from the bread box. Pumpkin, pineapple, and apple empanadas (pages 253-55) were always a favorite.

The recipes in this chapter remind me of this simpler time we spent breaking bread and strengthening our family ties.

### Pastel de Piña Colada
# PIÑA COLADA PIE
#### ·• Serves 8 •·

*This is an easy low-calorie dessert, great for a special occasion. Take care to avoid premade pie crusts that contain tropical oils or saturated fats.*

3¼ cups (245 g) light whipped topping

1¾ cups (455 g) low-fat coconut-flavored Greek yogurt,
preferably "toasted coconut vanilla"

1 cup (195 g) drained canned crushed pineapple

1 store-bought graham cracker pie crust

Mix together the whipped topping, yogurt, and pineapple in a large bowl. Spoon the mixture into the crust. Cover tightly and freeze overnight. Allow to soften slightly before serving.

———————

Per serving:
CALORIES 238; FAT 9 g (sat 5 g); PROTEIN 6 g; CARB 29 g; FIBER 1 g;
SUGARS 16 g; SODIUM 154 mg

## Papaya Fresca con Yogur de Frambuesa

# FRESH PAPAYA WITH RASPBERRY YOGURT

**← · Serves 2 · →**

*Papaya is rich in vitamins A and C. Try using a vanilla bean frozen yogurt or mango sorbet to fill the papaya for a great summer dessert.*

1 papaya, halved and seeded

1¼ cups (225 g) low-fat raspberry frozen yogurt, softened

½ cup (75 g) frozen raspberries

1 tablespoon sugar

**1.** Fill the papaya halves with the frozen yogurt, then place in the freezer overnight.

**2.** In a blender or food processor, puree the raspberries and sugar. Strain to remove seeds, if desired. Transfer to a covered container and refrigerate until ready to serve.

**3.** Just before serving, remove the papaya from the freezer. Remove the skin and transfer each papaya half to a plate. Drizzle with the raspberry sauce and serve immediately.

———

Per serving:
CALORIES 272; FAT 2 g (sat 1 g); PROTEIN 6 g; CARB 58 g; FIBER 5 g;
SUGARS 43 g; SODIUM 103 mg

# Mangos y Fresas con Crema
# MANGOES AND STRAWBERRIES WITH CREAM
### ← · Serves 4 · →

*This recipe is very high in vitamins A and C from the mangoes and strawberries. Mangoes not ripe enough? Keep them in a cool, dark room for a few days and wait until they're slightly soft to the touch and have a sweet aroma. Buy mangoes when they are in season and enjoy them throughout the year by peeling, slicing, and freezing them.*

1 cup (245 g) low-fat vanilla yogurt

1 tablespoon brown sugar, or to taste

2 teaspoons almond extract

2 large mangoes

4 large strawberries

¼ cup (25 g) slivered almonds, toasted

Mint leaves (optional)

**1.** Mix together the yogurt, sugar, and almond extract in a small bowl until smooth. Divide evenly among four plates, forming a circle on each plate.

**2.** Peel and pit the mangoes, then cut each lengthwise into eight slices. Arrange four slices in a sunburst pattern on each plate.

**3.** In a blender or food processor, puree the strawberries. Pour the strawberry puree in the center of the plates with the mangoes. Garnish with the almonds and mint leaves, if desired.

**Fruta en Crema de Amaretto/Fruit in Amaretto Cream:** Instead of the almond extract, use 1½ tablespoons amaretto liqueur. You can also dollop the cream on 5 cups (825 g) sliced strawberries, mango pieces, or other chopped mixed fruit served simply in dessert glasses or bowls.

———

Per serving:
CALORIES 192; FAT 4 g (sat 1 g); PROTEIN 5 g; CARB 34 g; FIBER 3 g; SUGARS 30 g; SODIUM 40 mg

## Agua Fresca de Sandía
# WATERMELON AGUA FRESCA
**➤· Makes 6 cups (1.4 L ·➤**

*Watermelon agua fresca is a refreshing summer drink that contains potassium and vitamin C. You can use almost any type of fruit to make agua fresca. If you choose a fruit with seeds, it's best to strain the juice before serving. Depending on the type of fruit you choose, you may not even need to add the sugar.*

4 cups (600 g) cubed seedless watermelon

¼ cup (60 ml) fresh lime juice

2 tablespoons superfine sugar (optional)

Lime slices

**1.** Place the watermelon, lime juice, 4 cups (960 ml) water, and the sugar, if using, in a blender and blend well. Strain through a fine-mesh strainer.

**2.** Refrigerate for 1 hour or until well chilled. Serve in a glass filled with ice and garnish with a slice of lime.

———

Per serving (without sugar):
CALORIES 35; FAT 0 g (sat 0 g); PROTEIN 1 g; CARB 8 g; FIBER 1 g;
SUGARS 7 g; SODIUM 2 mg

## Gelatina de Mango
# MANGO MOLD
**⤙· Serves 8 ·⤚**

*This wonderful, easy mango dessert can be prepared in advance and made in individual molds so that it looks pretty when served. Garnish with fresh fruit of your choice.*

Two 0.3-ounce (8.5 g) packages sugar-free orange-flavored gelatin

One 0.3-ounce (8.5 g) package sugar-free lemon-flavored gelatin

1 cup (240 ml) boiling water

8 ounces (227 g) neufchatel cream cheese, cubed

1 cup (165 g) diced mango

Mango slices, strawberries, and/or raspberries (optional)

**1.** Pour the gelatin and boiling water into a blender. Remove the blender lid's center insert, place a clean kitchen towel over the blender opening, and blend until the gelatin dissolves. Add the cream cheese and diced mango and blend until smooth.

**2.** Pour into a mold or other container and refrigerate until set, about 3 hours. Garnish with mango slices, if desired, before serving.

––––––––

Per serving:
CALORIES 93; FAT 6 g (sat 4 g); PROTEIN 4 g; CARB 4 g; FIBER 0 g;
SUGARS 3 g; SODIUM 175 mg

## Gelatina Tropical
# TROPICAL FRUIT MOLD
### ✐· Serves 8 ·✐

*If you've got a sweet tooth, this is a great low-calorie dessert. It's good enough for company!*

Two 0.3-ounce (8.5 g) packages sugar-free orange-
flavored gelatin

2 cups (480 ml) boiling water

1½ cups (360 ml) guava nectar

1 mango, peeled, pitted, and diced

**1.** Dissolve the gelatin in the boiling water in a medium bowl. Add the guava nectar and stir to combine. Pour into dessert glasses or bowls and refrigerate until slightly thickened, 45 to 60 minutes.

**2.** Stir in the mango and refrigerate until firm, about 3 hours. Serve cold.

———

Per serving:
CALORIES 56; FAT 0 g (sat 0 g); PROTEIN 1 g; CARB 12 g; FIBER 0 g;
SUGARS 10 g; SODIUM 57 mg

# Galletas Merengue de Chocolate Mexicano
# MEXICAN CHOCOLATE MERINGUES

### ❧· Makes 36 meringues ·☙

*If you just want a little something sweet after your delectable Mexican meal, these meringues are perfect. They are baked with Mexican chocolate, which has a wonderful cinnamon flavor. They keep for about two weeks when stored in an airtight container.*

2 large egg whites

¼ teaspoon cream of tartar

Pinch of salt

½ cup (100 g) sugar, superfine if possible

1 teaspoon clear Mexican vanilla extract

⅓ cup (60 g) finely chopped Mexican chocolate, such as Abuelita (see Notes)

**1.** Preheat the oven to 225°F (100°C). Line a baking sheet with parchment paper.

**2.** Beat the egg whites in a large bowl at medium speed with a mixer until soft peaks form (see Notes).

**3.** Add the cream of tartar and salt. Keep beating until the mixture looks glossy, then slowly add the sugar, 1 teaspoon at a time. Once the sugar has been incorporated, add the vanilla. When stiff peaks form, fold in the chocolate.

**4.** Use a large star tip or drop the mixture by teaspoonfuls onto the prepared baking sheet. Make a small peak on each cookie.

**5.** Bake for 1 hour, then turn off the oven and leave the cookies in the warm oven for 1 more hour. Store in an airtight container.

**Notes:** *If using a star tip to pipe the meringues, make sure to chop the chocolate into pieces small enough to fit through. The chocolate tends to break, so use a sharp knife.*

*It's essential that the bowl and beaters are free of any trace of fat or grease. Any grease in the bowl will interfere with the egg whites beating properly.*

––––––––

Per serving (2 meringues):
CALORIES 39; FAT 1 g (sat 0 g); PROTEIN 1 g; CARB 8 g; FIBER 0 g;
SUGARS 6 g; SODIUM 14 mg

· · · · · · · · · · · · · · · · · · · · · · · · · **HEALTHY EASY MEXICAN** · · · · · · · · · · · · · · · · · · · · · · · · ·

240

Yogur Helado con Salsa de Mango y Limón

# FROZEN YOGURT WITH MANGO-LIME TOPPING

### ⭢ Serves 6 ⭢

*Mangoes are available year-round in the United States. My favorite mango is the Kent, which is creamy and flavorful. This recipe calls for key limes, but regular limes work, too. You can make the mango topping a day in advance and prepare the dessert just before serving. Add bananas to the bottom of the serving dish to make it even more special.*

**MANGO-LIME TOPPING**

½ cup (120 ml) fresh key lime juice, from about 20 key limes (see Notes)

¼ cup (50 g) sugar, or to taste (see Notes)

4 mangoes, peeled, pitted, and cubed

**YOGURT**

3 cups (525 g) low-fat vanilla frozen yogurt

2 tablespoons slivered almonds, toasted

**1.** To make the topping, pour the lime juice, sugar, and ¼ cup (60 ml) water into a heavy skillet and stir to combine. Add the mangoes and cook over medium heat until the syrup has reduced slightly, about 10 minutes. Place in a covered container and refrigerate for several hours.

**2.** Just before serving, spoon ½ cup (85 g) of the frozen yogurt into each dessert dish. Divide the mangoes evenly among the dishes. Top each with 1 teaspoon of the almonds.

**Notes:** *To make a simpler mango sauce, omit the lime juice and blend the sugar and mangoes in a food processor or blender until smooth instead of cooking it. This sauce is also delicious drizzled over oatmeal, strawberries, bananas, or frozen yogurt. You can even freeze it for later use.*
*The sugar can be substituted with the equivalent amount of sugar substitute, if desired.*

————

Per serving:
CALORIES 273; FAT 3 g (sat 1 g); PROTEIN 5 g; CARB 60 g; FIBER 3 g;
SUGARS 49 g; SODIUM 79 mg

## Pudín de Kahlúa con Frambuesas

# KAHLÚA PARFAIT WITH RASPBERRIES

**◄·· Serves 4 ·►**

*This dessert is low in sugar and an excellent choice for diabetics. The Kahlúa adds just a touch of coffee flavor! Top with chocolate curls for a special touch.*

2 cups (480 ml) skim milk

One 1.4-ounce (39 g) package sugar-free chocolate instant pudding

1 tablespoon Kahlúa

½ cup (35 g) light whipped topping (optional)

½ cup (75 g) frozen raspberries, slightly thawed

**1.** Pour the milk, pudding mix, and Kahlúa into a medium bowl. Whisk until smooth, about 2 minutes. Divide the mixture among four dessert glasses or bowls.

**2.** Refrigerate for at least 1 hour. Top with the whipped topping, if using, and the raspberries before serving.

———

Per serving:
CALORIES 109; FAT 1 g (sat 1 g); PROTEIN 5 g; CARB 18 g; FIBER 2 g; SUGARS 10 g; SODIUM 325 mg

# Flan de Mango
# MANGO FLAN
## ← · Serves 6 · →

*The calories in this version of a favorite Mexican dessert are much lower than the original, because this one is prepared with evaporated milk, less sugar, and no cream cheese or sweetened condensed milk. Mango puree gives this dessert the essence of the fruit with fewer calories. Serving flan in individual ramekins and topping with fresh strawberries, sliced mango, and toasted nuts makes it quite elegant.*

1 tablespoon butter/oil blend, such as Land O'Lakes butter with olive oil

One 12-ounce (354 ml) can evaporated milk

3 large eggs, beaten

½ cup (120 ml) mango puree

1 teaspoon clear Mexican vanilla extract

½ teaspoon lemon zest

½ cup (100 g) plus ⅓ cup (65 g) sugar

Fresh berries, mango slices, and/or toasted sliced almonds (optional)

**1.** Preheat the oven to 325°F (165°C). Lightly grease six ramekins with the butter.

**2.** Place the milk, eggs, mango puree, vanilla, lemon zest, and ⅓ cup (65 g) of the sugar in a blender and blend until smooth. Set aside.

**3.** Place the remaining ½ cup (100 g) sugar in an 8-inch (20 cm) heavy nonstick skillet over medium-low heat and cook until the sugar liquefies and turns an amber-brown color, 10 to 13 minutes. Shake the pan gently, watching carefully to prevent burning. Remove from the heat immediately after the sugar caramelizes and most of the lumps are gone.

**4.** While the sugar is caramelizing, heat 3 to 4 cups (720 to 960 ml) water and simmer while preparing the flan.

**5.** Place the ramekins in a 9 x 13-inch (23 x 33 cm) baking dish. Working quickly, divide the caramelized sugar evenly among ramekins (about 1½ tablespoons in each one), covering the bottoms. If the sugar solidifies, heat it gently so you can pour it into the ramekins.

**6.** Divide the blended mixture evenly among the ramekins. Pour enough of the hot water into the baking dish to come halfway up the sides of the ramekins. Bake for about 50 minutes, until the flans are almost set and move only slightly when shaken gently. Remove the ramekins from the water. Cool slightly, then chill, uncovered, overnight.

**7.** To serve, run a knife around the ramekin edges and invert the flan onto a plate, shaking gently to allow the custard to settle on the plate. You may have to place the ramekins in a container with hot water to loosen the flan before inverting it. Top with the berries, mango, and/or almonds, if desired.

――――――

Per serving:
CALORIES 258; FAT 9 g (sat 4 g); PROTEIN 8 g; CARB 38 g; FIBER 0 g;
SUGARS 36 g; SODIUM 114 mg

## Peras con Dulce de Leche
# PEARS WITH DULCE DE LECHE
### ◆· Serves 6 ·◆

*Dulce de leche, a caramel-like topping made from milk, is creamy and rich. It's used in many Latin American dessert recipes, such as cookies, pies, and cakes. In this recipe, it is warmed and added in a light drizzle over yummy baked pears. You can buy a squeeze bottle of dulce de leche in the baking section of the grocery store that is just perfect for that little drizzle! A small amount provides lots of flavor.*

4 tablespoons butter/oil blend, such as Land O'Lakes butter with olive oil

1½ teaspoons ground cinnamon

1 teaspoon clear Mexican vanilla extract

6 Bosc pears, halved, stemmed, and cored

1½ cups (360 ml) apple juice

1 tablespoon dulce de leche, slightly warmed

**1.** Preheat the oven to 350°F (180°C).

**2.** Mix the butter, cinnamon, and vanilla in a small bowl to form a paste. Use your hands to cover each pear half with the mixture.

**3.** Place the pears face down in a baking dish. Pour in ¾ cup (180 ml) of the apple juice. Bake for 25 minutes, then remove from the oven and flip the pears so that the cut side faces up. Add the remaining apple juice and bake for about 20 minutes, until the pears are tender. Remove from the oven and allow to cool slightly.

**4.** Just before serving, drizzle the dulce de leche over the pears.

———

Per serving:
CALORIES 199; FAT 7 g (sat 3 g); PROTEIN 1 g; CARB 34 g; FIBER 4 g;
SUGARS 25 g; SODIUM 69 mg

## Plátanos con Canela

# BANANAS IN CINNAMON SAUCE

**Serves 4**

*If you have bananas on hand, try making this super simple dessert. Bananas are a good source of fiber as well as potassium.*

4 firm bananas, peeled

¼ cup (50 g) sugar

1 tablespoon plus 1 teaspoon butter/oil blend, such as Land O'Lakes butter with olive oil

½ teaspoon ground cinnamon

½ cup (50 g) slivered almonds, toasted

Low-fat vanilla frozen yogurt (optional)

**1.** Preheat the oven to 325°F (165°C).

**2.** Cut each banana in half crosswise, then in half lengthwise. Place in a baking dish.

**3.** Combine the sugar, butter, and cinnamon in a small bowl. Microwave for about 30 seconds, until the butter is melted, then stir to combine. Pour over the bananas.

**4.** Bake for about 15 minutes, basting frequently with the sauce, until the bananas turn golden brown.

**5.** Serve warm, topped with frozen yogurt, if desired.

---

Per serving (without yogurt):
CALORIES 265; FAT 10 g (sat 2 g); PROTEIN 4 g; CARB 43 g; FIBER 5 g;
SUGARS 34 g; SODIUM 32 mg

## Crujiente de Mango y Manzana
# MANGO AND APPLE CRISP
#### ← · Serves 8 · →

*This crisp can be adapted to include any combination of fruits on hand. Often, baked fruit desserts are made with butter or shortening. This recipe is prepared with oil, making it low in saturated fat. I love this combination of apples and mango, but you can also use apples and reduced-sugar dried cranberries.*

Nonstick cooking spray

¾ cup (60 g) rolled oats

½ cup (110 g) brown sugar, packed

⅓ cup (40 g) all-purpose flour

3 tablespoons canola oil

½ teaspoon ground cinnamon

Pinch of salt

3 large tart apples (such as Granny Smith), peeled, cored, and diced

1 mango, peeled, pitted, and diced

Low-fat frozen yogurt (optional)

**1.** Preheat the oven to 350°F (180°C). Spray a pie pan with nonstick cooking spray.

**2.** Mix the oats, sugar, flour, oil, cinnamon, and salt in a medium bowl.

**3.** Place the apples and mango in the pie pan. Cover with the oat mixture and bake for about 30 minutes, until the oats have browned slightly. Serve with yogurt, if desired.

———

Per serving:
CALORIES 205; FAT 6 g (sat 1 g); PROTEIN 2 g; CARB 38 g; FIBER 3 g;
SUGARS 27 g; SODIUM 6 mg

### Crujiente de Fruta Mexicano

# MEXICAN FRUIT CRUMBLE

**➤• Serves 4 •➤**

*I love making warm fruit desserts during cool months. You can use peaches, blueberries, apples, or any seasonal fruit that can be baked to prepare this recipe.*

3 tablespoons granulated sugar

½ cinnamon stick, broken into pieces

3 cups (465 g) sliced peaches

2 tablespoons fresh lime juice

½ cup (60 g) all-purpose flour

¼ cup (55 g) brown sugar, packed

1 tablespoon canola oil

**1.** Preheat the oven to 375°F (190°C).

**2.** Place the granulated sugar and cinnamon stick in a blender and blend until the cinnamon stick has been completely mixed into the sugar, about 5 minutes. Stop and start the blender to make sure that the cinnamon has been completely pulverized.

**3.** Place the peaches in a pie pan and toss gently with the lime juice. Add the cinnamon sugar and toss again.

**4.** Bake for about 45 minutes, until the peaches have cooked through.

**5.** While the fruit bakes, combine the flour, brown sugar, and oil in a medium bowl with a fork until crumbly. Sprinkle on top of the baked fruit and bake for about 15 minutes, until the top is golden brown.

———

Per serving:
CALORIES 225; FAT 4 g (sat 0 g); PROTEIN 2 g; CARB 48 g; FIBER 3 g;
SUGARS 33 g; SODIUM 6 mg

Empanadas de Manzana

# APPLE EMPANADAS

**➤· Makes 12 small empanadas ·➤**

*There are so many different fillings for empanadas; any fruit that can be made into a pie can be used for these, not just apple. I like to dust empanadas with just a touch of turbinado sugar before baking. These are best eaten fresh out of the oven. Almost all pastries for pies and empanadas are made with butter, shortening, or even lard. This recipe is made with oil, which makes the pastry healthier. It's very simple to make; when baked, it's crispy and has added flavor from the cinnamon and cinnamon tea.*

**APPLE FILLING**

2 tablespoons cornstarch

3 Granny Smith apples, peeled, cored, and diced

½ cup (60 g) reduced-sugar dried cranberries

⅓ cup (65 g) granulated sugar

½ teaspoon clear Mexican vanilla extract

**PASTRY**

Nonstick cooking spray

2 cups (240 g) all-purpose flour

1 teaspoon ground cinnamon

⅛ teaspoon salt

½ cup (120 ml) canola or other vegetable oil

⅓ cup (80 ml) cinnamon tea, cooled (see Note)

¼ cup (60 ml) skim milk

Turbinado sugar, for dusting

**1.** To make the filling, mix the cornstarch and ½ cup (120 ml) water in a small bowl to form a slurry. Set aside.

**2.** Place the apples, cranberries, and sugar in a large pot and stir to combine. Add the cornstarch slurry and cook over medium heat, stirring often, until the apples are soft, about 10 minutes. Add the vanilla and stir to combine. Remove from the heat and let cool before using.

· · · · · · · · · · · · · · · · · · · · · · · · · · · · **DESSERTS** · · · · · · · · · · · · · · · · · · · · · · · · · · ·

253

**3.** To make the pastry, preheat the oven to 350°F (180°C). Spray a baking sheet with cooking spray or line with parchment paper.

**4.** Whisk together the flour, cinnamon, and salt in a medium bowl. Add the oil and cinnamon tea and mix until crumbly. Bring the dough together with your hands and gently, without kneading too much, form a ball. Add a little flour if the dough is too sticky. Cut the dough ball in half, then form six smaller balls from each half.

**5.** Place a large sheet of waxed paper on a moistened work surface (so that the waxed paper doesn't move around too much). Place one dough ball on the paper, then place another piece of waxed paper on top. Roll into a circle 4 to 5 inches (10 to 13 cm) in diameter.

**6.** Place the filling on the lower half of the dough circle, then fold it over in half. Pinch the edges together tightly using your fingers to make indentations. Pierce each empanada three times with the tip of a very sharp knife to release steam. Brush the top of each empanada with milk and sprinkle a small amount of sugar on top. Bake for 18 to 20 minutes, until golden brown.

**Note:** *Prepare cinnamon tea by breaking 1 or 2 fresh cinnamon sticks in half and boiling them with 2 cups (480 ml) water in a saucepan. Lower the heat and allow to simmer for 15 to 20 minutes, to your desired strength. Strain to remove the cinnamon sticks.*

———

Per serving (1 empanada):
CALORIES 232; FAT 9 g (sat 1 g); PROTEIN 2 g; CARB 35 g; FIBER 2 g;
SUGARS 16 g; SODIUM 27 mg

**Empanadas de Mango/Mango Empanadas:** Instead of the apple filling, use one recipe Mango-Lime Topping (page 242). Let cool before using.

———

Per serving (1 empanada):
CALORIES 224; FAT 9 g (sat 1 g); PROTEIN 3 g; CARB 33 g; FIBER 2 g;
SUGARS 16 g; SODIUM 28 mg

**Empanadas de Calabaza/Pumpkin Empanadas:** Combine 1 cup (240 g) canned pumpkin puree, ¼ cup (50 g) granulated sugar, 1 teaspoon ground cinnamon, ½ teaspoon ground ginger, and ½ teaspoon clear Mexican vanilla extract. Let cool and use in place of the apple filling.

———

Per serving (1 empanada):
CALORIES 185; FAT 9 g (sat 1 g); PROTEIN 2 g; CARB 23 g; FIBER 1 g;
SUGARS 6 g; SODIUM 75 mg

**Empanadas de Piña/Pineapple Empanadas:** Combine 1 cup (250 g) crushed pine-apple in juice, ¼ cup (50 g) granulated sugar, 2½ tablespoons cornstarch, 1 table-spoon fresh lemon juice, and ½ teaspoon ground cinnamon in a medium saucepan. Cook over medium heat until the mixture thickens. Let cool and use in place of the apple filling.

———

Per serving (1 empanada):
CALORIES 260; FAT 9 g (sat 1 g); PROTEIN 2 g; CARB 42 g; FIBER 1 g;
SUGARS 24 g; SODIUM 29 mg

Pudín de Piña Colada

# PIÑA COLADA PUDDING

### ►· Serves 4—

*Children will love this pudding recipe. The flavors are fun and, because it's prepared with milk, it's a great source of calcium. Serve it in individual dessert glasses topped with a cherry for a special treat!*

One 4-serving package sugar-free vanilla instant pudding

2 cups (480 ml) skim milk

1 teaspoon coconut extract

1 cup (195 g) drained canned crushed pineapple

Maraschino cherries (optional)

Whisk together the instant pudding and skim milk until thickened, about 2 minutes. Add the coconut extract, then fold in the pineapple. Pour into dessert glasses or bowls and refrigerate for at least 1 hour. Garnish with cherries, if desired, and serve cold.

———

Per serving:
CALORIES 95; FAT 0 g (sat 0 g); PROTEIN 4 g; CARB 19 g; FIBER 1 g;
SUGARS 13 g; SODIUM 334 mg

# ACKNOWLEDGMENTS

This book is dedicated to my mother, Aida Garza, who showed her love for her family in many ways, but especially with food. She taught me to embrace the foods that were part of our culture and to prepare them well. Without her, this book would have not been possible.

I would like to thank Jorge, my husband of many years, who fell in love with my enchiladas and me, and our children, Christina, Jorge Jr., and Laura, who were the original taste testers of these recipes and who have become excellent cooks themselves. I would also like to thank Linda Hachfeld, MPH, RDN, the publisher of the first edition of this book, who believed in my idea and helped me share my culture and commitment to a healthy community with others. Thank you to Olivia Peluso and the amazing team at The Experiment: Beth Bugler, Matthew Lore, Zach Pace, Jeanne Tao, and Justin Walker.

Many thanks also to Elida Garza; Maria Olivia Garza, RD, RDN; Marlen Garza; Kathy Morin, RN; Francis Garza, RN; Laura Kinzel, MS, RDN; Sandy Tovar, DNP, PNP; Margaret Briley, PhD, RD, LD; Dolores Gutierrez; Alejandra Vela; Lucille de la Garza; Ellen Crouse; Lilia Cerna; Melissa Garcia; Mary Ella Garcia; Maricela Gomez; Myrna Rodriguez; Yali Manoharan; and Alejandra Cerna. Special thanks to my dear friend and photographer Diana Cantu, who took the lovely photo of me for this book.

# INDEX

Page numbers in *italics* refer to photos.

· · · · · · · · · · · · · · · · · · · · · · · · · · · · **HEALTHY EASY MEXICAN** · · · · · · · · · · · · · · · · · · · · · ·

260

· · · · · · · · · · · · · · · · · · · · · · · · · · **HEALTHY EASY MEXICAN** · · · · · · · · · · · · · · · · · · · · · · · · · ·

262

# ABOUT THE AUTHOR

**VELDA DE LA GARZA** is a registered dietitian whose Mexican heritage gives her firsthand knowledge of Mexican cuisine. Even as a young girl, Velda enjoyed cooking for her family and learning about traditional foods from her grandmother, great aunts, mother, and father. Using her knowledge of nutrition in combination with her love of cooking, she has compiled healthy versions of these much-loved Mexican foods.

Velda received her bachelor's degree in nutrition from the University of Texas at Austin and completed a dietetic internship at the Saint Marys Campus of the Mayo Clinic Hospital in Rochester, Minnesota. She received a master of science degree in nutrition from Texas Woman's University.

Velda has taught classes in heart-healthy eating in association with the office of McAllen Heart Surgeons. She was also a lecturer and instructor at the University of Texas–Pan American. She has previous experience as a dietitian at numerous hospitals, including the University of Texas MD Anderson Cancer Center in Houston. She has also worked as a consultant for the University of Texas Health Science Center at Houston and as a renal dietitian specialist. Her articles on food and nutrition have been published in *Latina* and *Cooking Light*. She and her husband, Jorge, a retired cardiothoracic surgeon, are the authors of *Heart to Heart: A Guide for Your Care After Open Heart Surgery.* She lives in McAllen, Texas.